the little, brown essential handbook for writers

Second Canadian Edition

Jane E. Aaron New York University

Elaine Bander Dawson College

PEARSON
Longman

Toronto

National Library of Canada Cataloguing in Publication

Aaron, Jane E.
    The Little, Brown essential handbook for writers / Jane E. Aaron,
Elaine Bander.

2nd Canadian ed.
Includes index.
ISBN 0-321-19994-4

1. English language—Grammar—Handbooks, manuals, etc.
2. English language—Rhetoric—Handbooks, manuals, etc.
I. Bander, Elaine, 1946– II. Title.

PE1112.A27 2005   808'.042   C2003-906271-6

ISBN 0-321-19994-4

Vice-President, Editorial Director: Michael J. Young
Executive Acquisitions Editor: Jessica Mosher
Marketing Manager: Toivo Pajo
Supervising Developmental Editor: Suzanne Schaan
Production Editor: Charlotte Morrison-Reed
Copy Editor: Ann McInnis
Proofreader: Heather Bean
Production Coordinator: Anita Heyna
Page Layout: Susan Thomas
Art Director: Julia Hall
Cover and Interior Design: Susan Thomas

3 4 5   09 08 07 06 05

Printed and bound in Canada.

PEARSON
Longman

Contents

This quick-reference outline lists all the book's topics and their page numbers. The symbol ESL *indicates material especially for writers using English as a second language.*

v

Using This Book

This little book contains essential information for writers in and out of school. Clarity and style, grammar, punctuation, mechanics, source documentation, usage—all the basics appear in a convenient, accessible format. (To see how the book works, look at the visual guide inside the back cover.) Explanations consider writers who are unfamiliar with the terminology of writing: needless terms are omitted, and essential terms, marked °, are defined in the Glossary of Terms. Material especially for writers using English as a second language is marked ESL. Examples come from a wide range of subjects, science to literature to business.

This book aims to support you in developing, documenting and editing your writing. Documenting sources helps make your writing informative and honest. Editing helps make it clear and effective—in other words, helps it *communicate*. For editing, you'll never need or use everything in this book because you already know much of what's here, whether consciously or not. The trick is to figure out what you *don't* know, focus on those areas, and back yourself up with this book. Discover what the book has to offer by scanning the Contents inside the front cover. If you can't find what you're looking for, use the Index. Keep a list of mistakes and other writing problems that your readers point out to you. This list can be your personal editing checklist, setting your priorities. When using the checklist, don't try to find every mistake in a single reading: you may need to read once for repetition, say, and once for apostrophes. And read with your own eyes: don't depend too much on your computer's grammar or spell-checker because neither can catch every error (a spell-checker, for instance, can't distinguish between *no, not,* and *now*).

Editing your writing is important, but it occurs in a larger context. That's why the first thing you see inside the front cover is a Writer's Checklist covering the entire process of writing. Contrary to much popular opinion, writing is *not* solely, or even primarily, a matter of correctness. True, any written message will find a more receptive audience if it is correct in grammar, punctuation, and similar matters. But these should come late in the process, after you've allowed yourself to discover what you want to say and how you want to say it, freeing yourself to make mistakes along the way. As one writer put it, you need to get the clay on the potter's wheel before you can shape it into a bowl, and you need to shape the bowl before you can perfect it. So get your clay on the wheel and work with it until it looks like a bowl.

I Writing and Speaking

Revision Checklist

✓Purpose

What is the paper's purpose? Does it conform to the assignment? Will it be clear to readers?

✓ Thesis

What is the thesis? Does the paper demonstrate it? What does each paragraph and each sentence contribute to the thesis? If there are digressions, should they be cut or reworked?

✓ Organization

What are the major points supporting the thesis? (List them.) How effective is their arrangement for the paper's purpose? Does the paper flow smoothly so that readers will follow easily?

✓ Development

How well do facts, examples, and other evidence support each major point and the thesis as a whole? Will readers find the paper convincing?

✓ Tone

Is the paper appropriately formal or informal for its readers? Does it convey your attitude appropriately—for instance, is it neither too angry nor too flippant?

✓ Use of Sources

Have you used sources to support, not substitute for, your own ideas? Have you integrated borrowed material into your own sentences? (See pp. 129–41).

✓ Title, introduction, and conclusion

Does the title convey the paper's content accurately and interestingly? Does the introduction engage and focus readers' attention? Does the conclusion provide a sense of completion?

✓ Format

Does the format of your paper suit your purpose and your audience's likely expectations for such papers?

1 The Process of Writing

WRITING is a way of discovering, recording, refining, and organizing your thoughts—hence a process—as well as a tool for communicating your thoughts in a rhetorical form that others can read and assimilate—hence a product. One of those rhetorical forms, the formal or academic essay, communicates facts, ideas, and interpretations. It normally has three main divisions:

- The *introduction* motivates your readers, establishes your topic, and states your thesis or main idea.
- The *body* contains the arguments, evidence, and illustrations, organized by topics into paragraphs, with which you persuade readers of the validity of your thesis or main idea.
- The *conclusion* briefly reinforces or restates your thesis or main idea and provides closure for your readers.

This essay structure may be adapted to other writing tasks such as reports, reviews, exam questions, memos, and letters; it is even adaptable to some non-writing tasks such as public speaking (see Chapter 2: Speaking and Listening). Thus, while this chapter addresses the process of writing an academic essay, it may help you with other writing and speaking tasks as well.

Clear, concise, cogent writing is the result of a great deal of thought, planning, writing, and rewriting. Books like this necessarily describe the writing process as an orderly progression of tasks broken down into separate, sequential steps. In reality, writers move back and forth from one step to another as ideas develop and change in response to research, thinking, writing, and revision. You too will find yourself moving back and forth between these steps as you engage in the writing process. Do not expect to discover, clarify, and communicate your ideas effectively in one or two drafts. Professional writers go through many drafts before they are satisfied, and so should you.

1a. Topic, audience, and purpose

Writing as an act of communication always occurs in a specific context. Your first task as a writer is to identify your TOPIC, your AUDIENCE, and your PURPOSE.

Topic

Some handbooks offer lengthy advice on how to select a topic. In real life, topics usually select us. For example, assume that your instructor assigns an essay on daycare in Canada. This topic is rather broad and could be approached in various ways. The assigned length will give some indication of the breadth, depth, and detail required: a 3000-word research paper that you write over several weeks should cover a broader field and contain more detail than an 800-word essay that you write in class. You are usually expected to focus and limit an assigned topic to meet length and time requirements as well as to reflect your own interests. For example, "daycare in Canada" might become "daycare in rural Manitoba" or "Canadian daycare policy since 2000." Paradoxically, a narrowly focused topic usually results in a more interesting essay than does a very general topic. If in doubt, consult your instructor.

When no topic is assigned, try freewriting and brainstorming exercises to discover your own ideas and interests. Narrow those broad ideas to a manageable topic that excites you. If you are passionate about your topic, you will find it easier to interest your readers.

For example, in thinking about the availability of daycare facilities in Canada, you might conclude that you are really interested in how families in rural Canada cope with childcare needs. Thus you could narrow the assigned general topic:

Daycare in Canada

to a more focused topic:

A Comparison of the Availability of Daycare Facilities in Urban and Rural Canada

This refocused topic gives you a personal handle on the general topic as well as a more manageable topic.

Audience

Anticipate your readers' familiarity with facts, documents, and opinions related to your topic, and consider how their knowledge, beliefs, and values may affect their responses to your facts and arguments. Do not assume that readers share your values and beliefs.

In academic essay writing, you are usually addressing an audience familiar with the subject matter in order to persuade readers that your presentation or analysis of the facts is valid. If you are writing a research paper, you are contributing to an ongoing conversation about the topic by a community of informed scholars, some of whom wrote generations ago and some of whom (like you) have only recently joined the discussion. You acknowledge the contributions of those who have preceded you while adding your own insights to the discussion (see Part VI: Research and Documentation).

A business report, in contrast, may circulate among several readers who have different degrees of familiarity with the topic, while a review article may discuss a text or performance with which your readers are not familiar. In each case, assess your audience's knowledge and needs.

Purpose

Is your purpose to convey information, stimulate debate, entertain readers, change their minds, or persuade them to act? Consider the wording of your assignment: terms like *compare*, *contrast*, *analyze*, *explain*, and *demonstrate* imply different logical approaches and should help you to determine your purpose. If in doubt, consult your instructor.

1b. Getting started

Prewriting

Good writing begins with PREWRITING. Brainstorming, freewriting, clustering, and other prewriting exercises stimulate you to think informally on paper or on a computer screen. They help you to discover

- what you already know or think about a topic
- which aspects of the topic most interest you
- what facts you need to learn in order to further develop your analysis

Jot down your ideas as fast as they come to you without stopping to censor them. Ask yourself questions about the topic: why? why not? when? how? who? what else? what if? how do I know this? how can I prove it? When stymied, stimulate your critical thinking by reading what others have written on the topic to see whether—or why—you agree. At this stage do not worry about neatness or grammatical correctness: no one will see these preliminary notes but you. Right now it is important to record your ideas; later you will work to shape them for readers.

Clusters of related thoughts, facts, and opinions should begin to emerge from your preliminary writing. Eventually these groupings will suggest main ideas or subtopics, generalizations or conclusions to present to your readers. They may also suggest areas needing further analysis or research (see chapters 36 and 37).

Your first jottings may look like this:

— Daycares—how many places avail. in cities?—how many in towns?—check StatsCan figures
— Urban pop. concentration: easier to org. daycares?—schools, churches, etc. avail. to use—small home daycares, etc. nearby
— Rural families: other resources available?—extended families?—neighbours?—need for daycare greater/lesser than urban families?
— Old days—young kids worked on farms—made economic contrib. to family—now??
— Effects of agribusiness on family farming? Both parents leaving home to work, like city folk—or not? Get stats on employment in/out of home.
— Rise of hobby farms, young families moving to country with city jobs—increased daycare need?

(1c.) Organizing your ideas

After further thought and research, group related ideas into subtopics. Eliminate any ideas or subtopics that do not fit your specific topic and purpose. However compelling and true, they do not belong in this essay.

You need not create a formal outline, but use *indentation* to show logical *subordination* so that facts and ideas appear indented under the broader ideas they support or illustrate:

— Cities: proportionately more daycare spaces than country
    — community, industry, gov't all provide
    — gov't subsidies

— Rural trends: fewer families, smaller families, less formal employment than in cities
    — organized, institutionalized daycare not practical:
        — irregular hours
        — lack of population density
        — distances, etc.

    — informal arrangements serve most needs, easier to establish than in cities
        — families

— friends, neighbours

— community org. (churches?)

If writing a research essay, identify areas requiring a further search of sources.

Note On a computer, save your preliminary notes and drafts in separate files. They may prove useful later in the writing process.

1d.   Developing and focusing your thesis

The main idea that emerges from prewriting activities and preliminary research provides a basis for constructing your THESIS STATEMENT. The thesis statement is the message that you wish your readers to receive after they have read your essay. It should be a complete sentence. If you are having trouble drafting a thesis statement, try to complete this sentence:

> After reading my essay, my readers will agree (or understand) that. . .

A possible thesis about daycare facilities in Canada based on preliminary writing might read

> More daycare facilities are available in urban areas than in rural areas.

Further research might confirm that this statement is true, but it is a weak thesis because it states a verifiable *fact* rather than a logically defended *opinion*. A strong thesis does more than *state* facts or generally held opinions. It *analyzes* or *interprets* facts:

Thesis   Although rural families do not have as much access to daycare facilities as do urban families, their informal arrangements adequately meet their childcare needs.

or

Thesis   Rural families, lacking adequate access to licensed daycares with trained staff, must entrust their children to risky and unregulated childcare arrangements.

Note that these two thesis statements interpret the same facts differently, but each should provoke readers to wonder, "How did you reach that conclusion?" A good thesis should take readers beyond a "So what?" shrug to a "Show me!" response.

A good thesis must also stand up to logical scrutiny and criticism. Is your thesis vulnerable to questions and contrary evidence? Anticipate your readers' reactions. For instance, you might ask

- How accurate are my statistics?
- How do I define a daycare facility?
- How are childcare facilities evaluated qualitatively?
- Have any studies shown whether licensed daycares provide better or safer environments than home childcare arrangements?

The answers to such questions help to focus, limit, or qualify your thesis so that you can better defend its validity. Revise your thesis as you refine your thinking.

Restricted or Aristotelian thesis

Some teachers advise you to write a RESTRICTED or ARISTOTELIAN THESIS. This is a thesis sentence that not only states your main idea but also includes your major supporting arguments:

Non-restricted thesis	The East Coast cod stocks may disappear forever.
Restricted or Aristotelian thesis	The East Coast cod stocks are in danger of disappearing because of overfishing by commercial factory trawlers, overdependence on the fish by inshore fishers and local processors, and rapid climate change.

A restricted thesis is very useful for writing essay exam questions or other short, impromptu compositions because the thesis serves as an outline or plan for what follows. Some instructors, however, discourage students from using a restricted thesis. Consult your instructor about his or her preferences.

(1e.) Developing arguments

A well-constructed thesis guides your selection and organization of arguments, evidence, and illustrations. To support the following thesis, for example, consider if any assumptions require further evidence:

Thesis	As government studies show, the proposed zoning change would put schoolchildren in the Redwood School District at risk by diverting high-speed traffic into local streets.

You might pose these questions:

- Are there any valid arguments against the government studies?
- What are the alleged dangers that the schoolchildren face?
- Are there other ways to reduce these dangers?
- Do the anticipated benefits of the proposed zoning change outweigh the potential dangers?

The answers to these questions might prompt you to modify (qualify) your thesis:

Revised thesis   As *some* government studies show, the proposed zoning change would put schoolchildren in the Redwood School District at risk by diverting high-speed traffic into local streets *unless other changes are also implemented.*

Clearly, in order to convince readers that this thesis is valid, you must first "prove" some other statements or assumptions on which the thesis depends:

- Studies conducted by the government and accepted by the City Council suggest that the proposed zoning changes will create new problems.
- Children will be at risk from increased high-speed traffic diverted from major arteries to the side streets around Riverside Elementary School.
- Changing the zoning for the East End district might reduce some of these dangers.

Each of these supporting ideas or subtopics becomes, in effect, a mini-thesis: the topic sentence of a BODY PARAGRAPH that develops and supports the thesis, and which in turn requires further development and support through facts, details, quotations, arguments, and illustrations to persuade readers that the topic sentence is valid, or to help readers visualize what you are describing.

1f.   Body paragraphs: unity, development, coherence

Unity

BODY PARAGRAPHS are like miniature essays. Each paragraph has a topic, usually expressed in a topic sentence. The topic sentence often begins the paragraph, but sometimes it occurs as a second or even concluding sentence of a paragraph, or it may even be implied rather than explicitly stated. The rest of the paragraph explains and supports the topic, using fact, argument, example, and so on. Nothing, however, should go into a paragraph that does not support the topic.

Development

1g

Body paragraphs may be developed using different organizing strategies or patterns. These include narration, description, process, definition, classification, example, comparison/contrast, cause-and-effect, problem/solution, and analogy. Body paragraphs often combine two or more of these patterns to develop their topics.

Strong paragraphs move from generalization to specific detail and, sometimes, back to generalization. Paragraphs whose sentences remain at the same level of abstraction as the topic sentence are not logically convincing: they simply restate or assert their topic rather than support or prove it. They lack development.

Coherence

Coherence refers to the logical flow of ideas and sentences. Good writers use verbal signposts to guide readers through their logic and to point to the direction that their arguments are leading. Use a TRANSITIONAL EXPRESSION° like *first*, *however*, *furthermore*, or *therefore* to show the logical relationship between sentence and sentence.

(1g.) Organizing arguments

Begin with your weakest or least interesting argument and build to your strongest:

Thesis   The East Coast cod stocks are seriously depleted and may disappear forever.

Topic sentences of body paragraphs

- Overfishing by commercial factory trawlers has severely depleted stocks.
- Economic overdependence on the fish by inshore fishers and local processors has put unsustainable pressure on the fish stocks.
- Unprecedented climate change may be killing the cod or driving them into more hospitable waters.

° The degree sign (°) marks every term defined in the Glossary of Terms, beginning on p. 198.

In revising this thesis, you may decide that your strongest argument is the one about factory trawlers while the weakest argument concerns climate change because the scientific evidence is controversial. Therefore you could reorder your body paragraphs to move from weakest to strongest:

- Unprecedented climate change may be killing the cod or driving them into more hospitable waters.
- Economic overdependence on the fish by inshore fishers and local processors has put unsustainable pressure on the fish stocks.
- Overfishing by commercial factory trawlers has severely depleted stocks.

1h. Writing the first draft

After devising a thesis statement and planning a strategy of development, writing the first draft is easy. Expand each paragraph so that it explains, illustrates, or defends the topic sentence for each subtopic, using selected detail and evidence to convince your readers. Add transitional expressions for coherence and logical clarity.

Note A fascinating fact or an elegant phrase belongs in a paragraph only if it supports your topic sentence, just as a paragraph belongs in an essay only if it supports your argument or purpose.

1i. Introductions and conclusions

Paragraphs that introduce and conclude an essay have special jobs to do and therefore take special forms.

Introductions

The introduction introduces readers to the thesis by gaining their attention, stating the topic, and setting the tone. An effective introduction usually begins broadly with an interesting statement about the topic intended to orient readers, then narrows quickly to a statement of the qualified or restricted thesis:

Governments frequently boast of the number of new daycare places they have made available to families. While these numbers may sound impressive, they obscure the fact that most daycares are located in urban or suburban areas. Rural families cannot make use of those well-publicized new places. Nevertheless, while rural families have less access to daycare facilities than do urban families, they also have less need. Traditional and non-traditional arrangements with family members and neighbours adequately provide for the child-care needs of most rural families.

Conclusions

Concluding paragraphs generally invert the structure of the introduction. Begin by briefly restating the thesis and, perhaps, summarizing your main arguments; then open out to a more general statement, a larger implication, or a desirable action that flows from the thesis:

Clearly, then, the daycare needs of rural families are adequately met at present by available facilities. As urbanization continues and family structures evolve, however, the needs of rural families may change as well. Governments should remember that what is sufficient today may yet prove inadequate tomorrow.

Note Until your rough draft is ready for revision and proofreading, do not worry about correctness. Concentrate on organizing your ideas and arguments and selecting your evidence and examples. Your draft is a tool of discovery, a work in progress.

1j. Revising your draft

Good writing emerges from successive revisions. Read your draft over several times for logical order, consistency, and unity, ensuring that each paragraph supports your thesis and that each sentence develops the paragraph's topic. Read critically, asking if statements are sufficiently supported by specific evidence. Add *transitional expressions*° to clarify the direction of your argument and permit the smooth flow of ideas.

On a computer, save successive revisions in separate files and make backup copies. Use key words with the *Find* and *Search* commands to move quickly to passages requiring revision. The outlining feature of many word processors is also a useful tool for analyzing your logical structure.

Referring to Part VI: Research and Documentation, make sure you have avoided plagiarism and acknowledged all sources according to the appropriate documentation style.

Revising for tone and diction

Academic writing requires *formal* or *standard* English. Avoid slang, dialect, and colloquialisms (see Chapter 6: Appropriate Words), contractions (see section 26c: Apostrophe with contractions), and first-person pronouns such as *I* and *we*.

(1k.) Editing your draft

Read your draft for logic and fluency, referring to the relevant chapters of this book to correct faulty or unclear sentences and to help you choose correct, concise expressions. On-screen editing can be difficult, so if using a word processor, print your draft for editing. Read your draft again for correct grammar, punctuation, spelling, and other mechanics, paying special attention to elements—for example, apostrophes—that you know you tend to misuse. Use a dictionary or thesaurus to double-check dubious or ambiguous word choices. On a computer, use *Find* and *Search* commands to locate words and phrases for which you commonly make errors. Refer to Part II: Clarity and Style and Part III: Sentence Parts and Patterns. Follow the formatting guidelines for the appropriate style in Chapter 29 in preparing your final copy.

(1l.) Proofreading your draft

PROOFREAD for spelling by reading your document backward from the last word to the first word, looking only at how each word is spelled. Never accept a computer spell-checker's suggestions uncritically. It may query a word correctly spelled according to Canadian, not American, spelling conventions (see Chapter 35: Spelling) or a word you have deliberately repeated. It will not, however, distinguish homonyms such as *whose* or *who's*, *their* or *there*, *sight* or *site* or *cite*, nor will it recognize a wrong or a missing word.

Proofread again, preferably out loud, reading forward slowly to correct any missing words, accidentally repeated words, or other typographical errors. Make necessary corrections neatly in ink for academic papers, but retype a page if it requires more than a few corrections. Retype to eliminate any errors for business communication.

2 Speaking and Listening

(2a.) Written vs. oral communication

Since listeners cannot skim or review a speech as they can an essay, oral communication requires a more explicit structure and greater use of repetition to compensate.

Organization: introduction, conclusion, transitions

Like an essay or report, a speech has an introduction, a body, and a conclusion. The introduction of a speech, however, provides a more explicit statement of the thesis (the statement of intention). It also features a preview of the organization of the speech (the division of the topic).

Use the introduction to set an appropriate tone and to establish a common purpose with the audience. Use more frequent and explicit transitional expressions° as well as more repetition in the form of summaries and previews. Use more signposting than you would when writing:

Written   Louis Riel was found guilty of high treason and hanged on 16 November 1885. Today many Canadians look upon him as a hero, a patriot, a founding father of the nation. Thus, a traitor for one age becomes a hero for another. Clearly, the way we interpret history depends on who we are and where we live.

Oral   On 16 November 1885, Louis Riel was found guilty of high treason and hanged, yet today many Canadians look upon him as a hero, a patriot, and a founding father of the nation. I want to talk to you about how we interpret history. Specifically, I'll discuss how our view of history depends on who we are and where we live. I'll look at the case of Louis Riel, show how opinions about him have evolved over the last century, and, finally, suggest some contemporary figures whose reputations may go through surprising changes before the year 2100.

| **Transition** | I'll begin by reminding you of the historical record of Riel and the North-West Rebellion. |

Signal the approach of your conclusion:

"Before concluding, I will add one further example . . ."

"To sum up . . ."

Visualization

Use vivid language and concrete examples to help your audience visualize what you are describing.

| **Not** | Among the schoolchildren in this city, 34.5 percent do not receive sufficient nourishment at breakfast and lunch. |
| **But** | Right now Alice is sitting in her Grade 3 classroom with a rumbling stomach. She'll go hungry at recess and lunch hour because her mum was out of peanut butter this morning. In our city's schools, every third child, like Alice, comes to school hungry. |

Audiovisual presentational aids are also useful.

Diction

Listeners cannot consult a dictionary or glossary. Unless you are addressing an audience of experts, avoid technical terms. Use a vocabulary appropriate to your audience. Avoid distracting slang, blasphemy, or profanity as well as obscure and difficult words. If you can't avoid terms that your audience may not know, define them (see Chapter 6).

Statistics

In oral delivery, round off statistics.

| **Not** | 48.73 percent of votes |
| **But** | nearly half the votes |

Documentation

Provide oral footnotes:

According to a recent Statistics Canada study, the population of our town is expanding.

The newly elected head of the CMA told *The Globe and Mail* last week that Canadian medical care is in crisis.

Note Be prepared to provide detailed citations if someone questions your sources.

2b. Oral delivery

Methods of oral delivery

Reading

Reading prevents effective eye contact and encourages a monotonous delivery. Avoid reading a prepared speech to an audience.

If you *must* read a speech, print it out in a large typeface, double-spaced, and add cues to remind yourself to smile at the audience, tell a joke, pause, slow down, or ask a question.

Memorization

A memorized speech can be deadly to listen to and deadlier to give, especially if your memory dries up. Unless you are an accomplished actor, a memorized delivery also sounds unnatural. Avoid memorizing a text for delivery.

Extemporaneous delivery

Extemporaneous public speaking is the most difficult form to master, but with practice it is the easiest and most effective to use. An extemporaneous speech is thoroughly researched, planned, and rehearsed, but it is not memorized, nor is it written out in sentences to be read.

Instead, speak from brief notes, preferably a few key words jotted down on cue cards to remind you of your next point. You are thus *thinking* about your ideas, not just *reciting* them. You are looking at your *audience*, not your *script*. Your sentences may not be as perfectly crafted as if you were reading—although with practice you will gain confidence and fluency—but what you lose in correctness you gain in communication with your audience. It's a worthwhile trade.

Techniques of oral delivery

Eye contact

Look at your audience. Sweep the room with your eyes. Glance briefly at your notes when necessary, but maintain regular eye contact.

Posture and body language

Assume a comfortable but dignified posture. Avoid leaning on a lectern, slouching, random arm waving, constant weight shifting, restless pacing. Do not chew gum, twirl hair, jangle bracelets, rustle notes, or click pens. Adjust your facial expression to the tone and content of your speech.

2b

Voice

Speak loudly enough to be heard without shouting. Vary your pitch and pace to avoid boredom. Avoid a singsong or repetitive inflection. Drop your voice, slow down, or pause occasionally for emphasis, but do not speak so slowly that listeners lose the thread of what you are saying. (Our minds process words faster than most speakers can say them.) Enunciate clearly, especially consonants. If necessary, exaggerate slightly for clarity.

2c

Presentational aids

Practise using overhead projectors, computer graphic displays, videotapes, or other presentational aids you intend to use in your speech. Cue tapes and check equipment, including focus and sound levels, before your speech begins. Introduce aids only when needed to illustrate your speech: explain their significance, then turn them off or put them away to avoid distracting your audience.

Confidence

Confidence comes with experience. Control stage fright in the following ways:

- **Breathing:** Breathe deeply to slow down an adrenaline rush.
- **Muscular relaxation:** Systematically flex and relax muscle groups to reduce tension before speaking.
- **Visualization:** Practise imagining yourself speaking eloquently to an appreciative audience.
- **Thorough preparation.**

If you lose your train of thought or make a mistake, keep talking: chances are the audience won't know you've made a mistake unless you tell them. If all else fails, summarize what you've said so far. You'll probably remember where your speech was heading, and you'll soon be back on track. Above all, remember that your listeners want you to succeed: they want to relax for the duration of your speech while you take charge.

2c. Listening

We spend many more hours listening in class, at work, and in social situations than we do speaking. Learn to be an effective listener:

- *Do not* fake listening while you are really thinking about something else, such as your response, or your shopping list.

- *Do not* prejudge the speaker or dwell on his or her speech defect or bad fashion sense.
- *Do not* let yourself be distracted by physical noise (a banging door, the scene outside the window), psychological noise (your private thoughts), or semantic noise (your misunderstanding of, or emotional reaction to, the speaker's choice of words).
- *Do* motivate yourself to listen by asking yourself, "What can this speaker teach or offer me?"
- *Do* concentrate on the sequence of ideas being presented, listening critically for details that logically support the ideas.
- *Do* take notes to help focus your attention.

We all perform better for a responsive audience. Good listeners encourage good speakers.

2c

II Clarity and Style

Checklist for Clarity and Style

✓**Emphasis**

Do the subjects and verbs of sentences focus on key actors and actions? (See p. 34.) Do the beginnings and endings of sentences stress main ideas and move from old information to new? (See p. 22.) Are equally important ideas linked through coordination? (See p. 21.) Are less important ideas de-emphasized through subordination? (See p. 22.)

✓ **Conciseness**

Have you used the active voice and otherwise focused subjects and verbs on key actors and actions? (See p. 34.) Have you cut empty words and unneeded repetition? (See pp. 134–35.) Have you recast unneeded *there is* and *it is* constructions? (See p. 36.) Have you reduced word groups to their essence and combined sentences where appropriate? (See p. 36.)

✓ **Parallelism**

Have you used parallel constructions to show the equivalence of elements connected by *and, or, not only . . . but, also,* and similar words? (See p. 124.)

✓ **Variety and details**

Have you varied sentence lengths and structures to stress your main ideas and hold readers' attention? (See p. 25.) Are your sentences well detailed so that readers will find them clear and interesting? (See p. 26.)

✓ **Appropriate words**

Is your language appropriate for your writing situation? (See pp. 27–29.) Have you avoided biased language? (See pp. 29–31.)

✓ **Exact words**

Are your words suited to your meaning and also concrete and specific? (See pp. 31–32.) Are your words correct in idiom and also fresh, not clichéd? (See p. 33.)

3 Coordination and Subordination

When clearly written, your sentences show the relationships between ideas and stress the more important ideas over the lesser ones. Two techniques, coordination and subordination, can help you achieve such clarity.

3a. Coordination for relationships

Use COORDINATION to show that two or more elements in a sentence are equally important in meaning.

- Link two complete sentences (main clauses°) with a comma and a coordinating conjunction° (*and, but, or, nor, for, so, yet*).

  The first Calgary Stampede in 1912 was a great success, <u>but</u> *a second one was not held until 1919.*

- Link two main clauses with a semicolon alone or a semicolon and a conjunctive adverb,° such as *however, indeed,* or *therefore.*

  The early Stampedes were cowboy shows; since 1923, <u>however</u>, *the Stampede has included an agricultural exhibition.*

- Within clauses, link words and word groups with a coordinating conjunction (*and, but, or, nor*) but no comma.

  Cowboys <u>and</u> *city folk alike flocked to the bronco riding* <u>or</u> *thronged the chuckwagon racing events.*

Coordination clarifies meaning and smooths choppy sentences.

Choppy sentences	We should not rely so heavily on oil. Coal and uranium are also overused. We have a substantial energy resource in the moving waters of our rivers. Smaller streams add to the total volume of water. The resource renews itself. Coal and oil are irreplaceable. Uranium is also irreplaceable. The cost of water does not increase much over time. The costs of coal, oil, and uranium rise dramatically.

Ideas coordinated   We should not rely so heavily on coal, oil, <u>and</u> uranium, <u>for</u> we have a substantial energy resource in the moving waters of our rivers <u>and</u> streams. Coal, oil, <u>and</u> uranium are irreplaceable <u>and</u> thus subject to dramatic cost increases; water, <u>however</u>, is self-renewing <u>and</u> more stable in cost.

Notes A string of main clauses connected by *and* implies that all ideas are equally important and creates a dull, plodding rhythm. Use subordination (see the next section) to revise such excessive coordination.

Two punctuation errors, the comma splice and the fused sentence, can occur when you link main clauses. See pp. 72–74.

(3b.) ## Subordination for emphasis

Use SUBORDINATION to indicate that some elements in a sentence are less important than others for your meaning. Usually, the main idea appears in the main clause,° and supporting information appears in subordinate structures such as the following:

- Subordinate clauses° containing a subject and a verb (like a complete sentence) but beginning with a subordinating word such as *although, because, before, if, since, that, when, where, which,* or *who* (*whom*).

  <u>*Although*</u> *production costs have declined,* they are still high. [Stresses that costs are still high.]

  Costs, <u>*which include labour and facilities,*</u> are difficult to control. [Stresses that costs are difficult to control.]

- Phrases.°

  Despite some decline, production costs are still high.

  Costs, *including labour and facilities,* are difficult to control.

- Single words.

  Declining costs have not matched prices.

  Labour costs are difficult to control.

Subordination can transform a monotonous string of main clauses into a more emphatic and interesting passage. (See also p. 25.)

String of   In recent years computer prices have
main clauses   fallen, and production costs have
                   fallen more slowly, and computer
                   manufacturers have had to struggle,
                   for their profits have been shrinking.

Revised   *Because* production costs have fallen
                   more slowly *than computer prices* in
                   recent years, computer manufactur-
                   ers have had to struggle *with shrink-*
                   ing profits.

Generally, subordinate clauses give the most emphasis to secondary information, phrases give less, and single words give the least.

Note A subordinate clause or a phrase is not a complete sentence and should not be set off and punctuated as one. See pp. 71–72 on sentence fragments.

4 Parallelism

PARALLELISM is a technique for matching the form of
your sentence to its meaning: when your ideas are
equally important, or parallel, you express them in similar, or parallel, grammatical form.

The air is dirtied by *factories belching smoke*
                          and
                      vehicles spewing exhaust.

To spot elements that should be parallel, look for
two or more words or phrases connected by coordinating conjunctions or correlative conjunctions, as shown
in the sections following.

Note Parallelism can work like glue to link and stress
the sentences of a paragraph as well as the parts of a
sentence: *Pulleys are ancient machines for transferring*
power. Unfortunately, they are also inefficient machines.

4a.   Parallelism with *and, but, or, nor, yet*

The coordinating conjunctions° *and, but, or, nor,* and *yet* signal a need for parallelism.

The industrial base is *shifting* <u>and</u> *shrinking.*

Politicians seldom *acknowledge the problem* <u>or</u> *propose alternatives.*

Industrial workers are understandably disturbed *that they are losing their jobs* <u>and</u> *that no one seems to care.*

Faulty   Three reasons why steel companies kept losing money were that their plants were inefficient, high labour costs, <u>and</u> foreign competition was increasing.

Revised   Three reasons why steel companies kept losing money were *inefficient plants, high labour costs,* and *increasing foreign competition.*

Note As the preceding example shows, parallel elements match in structure, but they need not match word for word.

Be careful not to omit needed words in parallel structures.

Faulty   Many workers find it difficult to have faith and work for the future.

Revised   Many workers find it difficult to have faith *in* and work for the future. [*Faith* and *work* require different prepositions,° so both must be stated.]

4b.   Parallelism with *both . . . and, either . . . or,* and so on

Correlative conjunctions° stress equality and balance between elements. Parallelism confirms the equality. The correlative conjunctions include *both . . . and, either . . . or, neither . . . nor, not only . . . but also,* and *whether . . . or.*

At the end of *The Stone Angel,* Hagar <u>both</u> *acknowledges her lifelong fear of love* <u>and</u> *affirms her feisty independence.*

With correlative conjunctions, the element after the second connector must match the element after the first connector.

Faulty	Hagar learns <u>not only</u> that love brings vulnerability <u>but also</u> comfort. [The first element includes *that love brings*; the second element does not.]
Revised	Hagar learns that love brings <u>not only</u> vulnerability <u>but also</u> comfort. [Repositioning *not only* makes the two elements parallel.]

5 Variety and Details

5a

To make your writing interesting as well as clear, use varied sentences that are well textured with details.

5a. Varied sentence lengths and structures

In most contemporary writing, sentences tend to vary from about ten to about forty words, with an average of fifteen to twenty-five words. If your sentences are all at one extreme or the other, your readers may have difficulty focusing on main ideas and seeing the relations among them.

- If most of your sentences contain thirty-five words or more, you probably need to break some of them into shorter, simpler sentences.
- If most of your sentences contain fewer than ten or fifteen words, you probably need to add details to them (next page) or combine them through coordination (p. 21) and subordination (p. 22).

A good way to hold readers' attention is to vary the structure of sentences so that they do not all follow the same pattern, like soldiers in a parade. Some suggestions:

- Enliven strings of main clauses° by subordinating the less important information (italics in the revision below).

Monotonous	The moon is now drifting away from the earth. It moves away at the rate of about one inch a year. Our days on earth are getting longer, and they grow a thousandth of a second longer every century.

A month will someday be forty-seven of our present days long, and we might eventually lose the moon altogether. Such great planetary movement rightly concerns astronomers, but it need not worry us. It will take 50 million years.

Revised   The moon is now drifting away from the earth *at the rate of about one inch a year. At a thousandth of a second or so every century,* our days on earth are getting longer. A month will someday be forty-seven of our present days long, *if we don't eventually lose the moon altogether.* Such great planetary movement rightly concerns astronomers, but it need not worry us. It will take 50 million years.

• Vary the beginnings of sentences so that some do not begin with their subjects.°

Monotonous   The lawyer cross-examined the witness for two days. The witness had expected to be dismissed within an hour and was visibly irritated. He did not cooperate. He was reprimanded by the judge.

Revised   *For two days,* the lawyer cross-examined the witness. *Expecting to be dismissed within an hour,* the witness was visibly irritated. He did not cooperate. *Indeed,* he was reprimanded by the judge.

• Occasionally, to achieve special emphasis, reverse the usual word order of a sentence.

A dozen witnesses testified, and the defence attorney barely questioned eleven of them. *The twelfth, however, he grilled.* [Compare normal word order: *He grilled the twelfth, however.*]

5b. Details

Relevant details such as facts and examples create the texture and life that keep readers awake and help them grasp your meaning. For instance:

Flat   Built in Montreal harbour, the former Expo 67 site is a popular place for sports and also features other attractions.

Detailed Built *on a green archipelago of natural and artificial islands* in Montreal harbour, the former Expo 67 site is a popular place for *walking, cycling, rollerblading, rowing, swimming, and ice skating,* and also features *international gardens, a casino, a theatre, and exhibits of national treasures from countries such as China and Macedonia.*

6 Appropriate Words

6a

English-speaking Canadians share a common language, but sometimes they speak it quite differently. Newfoundland English has a vocabulary, syntax, and pronunciation all its own. To a lesser extent, so does Quebec English, the English of the Ottawa Valley, and the English of the Prairies. Canadians who speak indigenous languages such as Cree, Mohawk, and Inuktitut may flavour their English with syntax and idiom borrowed from their languages. Canadians from many regional and ethnic backgrounds have enriched our common English language.

Nevertheless, most academic and business writing calls for *standard English*, usually defined as the English expected and used by educated English-speaking people. Therefore, in academic and business writing use regional and ethnic dialect words and phrases cautiously, only when you are aiming for a particular effect with a particular audience. In all cases, avoid words and expressions that your readers might find confusing, hurtful, or insulting.

6a. Slang

SLANG is the insider language used by a group, such as musicians or football players, to reflect common experiences and to make technical references efficient. The following example is from an essay on the slang of "skaters" (skateboarders):

> Curtis slashed ultra-punk crunchers on his longboard, while the Rube-man flailed his usual Gumbyness on tweaked frontsides and lofty fakie ollies.
>
> —MILES ORKIN, "Mucho Slingage by the Pool"

Though valuable within a group, slang is often too private or imprecise for academic or business writing.

6b. Colloquial language

COLLOQUIAL LANGUAGE is the everyday spoken language, including expressions such as *get together, go crazy,* and *do the dirty work.* It is labelled "informal" or "colloquial" in your dictionary.

Colloquial language suits informal writing, and an occasional colloquial word can help you achieve a desired emphasis in otherwise formal writing. But most colloquial language is not precise enough for academic or career writing.

6c. Dialect

Like many countries, Canada includes several regional, social, or ethnic groups that have their own distinct DIALECTS, or versions of standard English: standard English, Newfoundland English, West Indian English, and Ottawa Valley English are examples. English-speaking Quebecers frequently use words and expressions borrowed from French, giving their English a unique flavour.

If you normally speak a dialect version of English, be aware that in academic or business writing, where audiences usually expect standard English, your dialect words and expressions may be misunderstood or perceived as mistakes.

Edit your drafts to eliminate dialect expressions, especially those that dictionaries label "non-standard," such as *this here school, that there building, them books, knowed, throwed, eh, didn't ought, hadn't ought, didn't never, could of, would of, should of, didn't never, that house there, I'm allowed doing that, I think me, I done it, I seen it.*

6d. Jargon or technical words

All disciplines and professions rely on specialized language that allows the members to communicate precisely and efficiently with each other. Chemists, for instance, have their *phosphatides,* and literary critics have their *subtexts*. When writing to a non-specialist audience, avoid unnecessary technical terms and carefully define necessary terms.

6e. Indirect and pretentious writing

Small, plain, and direct words are usually preferable to big, showy, or evasive words. Take special care to avoid the following:

- EUPHEMISMS are presumably inoffensive words that substitute for words deemed potentially offensive or too blunt, such as *passed away* for *died* or *misspeak* for *lie*. Use euphemisms only when you know that blunt, truthful words would needlessly hurt or offend members of your audience.
- DOUBLE TALK (at times called DOUBLESPEAK or WEASEL WORDS) is language intended to confuse or to be misunderstood: the *revenue enhancement* that is really a tax, the *biodegradable* bags that last decades. Double talk has no place in honest writing.
- PRETENTIOUS WRITING is fancy language that is more elaborate than its subject requires. Choose your words for their exactness and economy. The big, ornate word may be tempting, but pass it up. Your readers will be grateful.

Pretentious   Many institutions of higher education recognize the need for youth at the threshold of maturity to confront the choice of life's endeavour and thus require students to select a field of concentration.

Revised   Many colleges and universities force students to make decisions about their careers by requiring them to select a major.

6f. Sexist and other biased language

Language can reflect and perpetuate inaccurate and hurtful prejudices toward groups of people, especially racial, ethnic, religious, age, and sexual groups. Insulting language communicates nothing but insult and reflects more poorly on the user than on the person or persons designated. Unbiased language does not submit to stereotypes. It refers to people as they would wish to be referred to.

Among the most subtle and persistent biased language is sexist language that distinguishes needlessly between men and women in such matters as behaviour, ability, temperament, occupation, and maturity. The following guidelines can help you eliminate sexist language from your writing:

• Avoid demeaning and patronizing language—for instance, identifying women and men differently or trivializing either gender.

Sexist	Like Tom Thomson, Emily painted the Canadian landscape.
Revised	Like Tom Thomson, *Emily Carr* painted the Canadian landscape.
Sexist	Ladies are entering almost every occupation.
Revised	*Women* are entering almost every occupation.

• Avoid occupational or social stereotypes, assuming that a role or profession is exclusively male or female.

Sexist	The considerate doctor commends a nurse when she provides his patients with good care.
Revised	The considerate doctor commends a nurse *who provides good care for patients*.

• Avoid using *man* or words containing *man* to refer to all human beings. Some alternatives:

businessman	businessperson
chairman	chair, chairperson
craftsman	craftsperson, artisan
layman	layperson
mankind	humankind, humanity, human beings, people
manpower	personnel, human resources
policeman	police officer
salesman	salesperson, sales representative

Sexist	Man has not reached the limits of social justice.
Revised	*Humankind* (or *Humanity*) has not reached the limits of social justice.
Sexist	The furniture consists of manmade materials.
Revised	The furniture consists of *synthetic* materials.

• Avoid using *he* to refer to both genders. (See also p. 59.)

Sexist	The newborn child explores his world.
Revised	The newborn child explores *his or her* world. [Male and female pronouns.]
Revised	Newborn *children* explore *their* world. [Plural.]
Revised	The newborn child explores *the* world. [Pronoun avoided.]

Referring to people with disabilities

Avoid defining people with disabilities as "disabled" or "handicapped."

| Offensive | Cripples can't climb those stairs. Handicapped people can't climb those stairs. Disabled students may apply for assistance. |
| Revised | People with mobility impairments can't climb those stairs. Those stairs handicap people with mobility impairments. Students with disabilities may apply for assistance. |

7a

Exact Words

To write clearly and effectively, you will want to find the words that fit your meaning exactly and convey your attitude precisely.

7a.   The right word for your meaning

One key to helping readers understand you is to use words according to their established meanings.

- Become acquainted with a dictionary. Consult it whenever you are unsure of a word's meaning.
- Distinguish between similar-sounding words that have widely different meanings.

| Inexact | Older people often suffer *infirmaries* [places for the sick]. |
| Exact | Older people often suffer *infirmities* [disabilities]. |

Some words, called HOMONYMS, sound exactly alike but differ in meaning: for example, *principal/principle* or *rain/reign/rein.* (Many homonyms and near-homonyms are listed in the Glossary of Usage, pp. 187–197.)

• Distinguish between words with related but distinct meanings.

Inexact   Television commercials *continuously* [unceasingly] interrupt programming.

Exact   Television commercials *continually* [regularly] interrupt programming.

• Distinguish between words that have similar basic meanings but different emotional associations, or CONNOTATIONS.

It is a *daring* plan. [The plan is bold and courageous.]

It is a *reckless* plan. [The plan is thoughtless and risky.]

Many dictionaries list and distinguish such SYNONYMS, words with approximately, but often not exactly, the same meanings.

7b

(7b.)   ## Concrete and specific words

Clear, exact writing balances abstract and general words, which outline ideas and objects, with concrete and specific words, which sharpen and solidify.

• ABSTRACT WORDS name qualities and ideas: *beauty, inflation, management, culture, liberal.* CONCRETE WORDS name things we can know by our five senses of sight, hearing, touch, taste, and smell: *sleek, humming, brick, bitter, musty.*
• GENERAL WORDS name classes or groups of things, such as *buildings, weather,* or *birds,* and include all the varieties of the class. SPECIFIC WORDS limit a general class, such as *buildings,* by naming one of its varieties, such as *skyscraper, Victorian courthouse,* or *hut.*

Abstract and general statements need development with concrete and specific details. For example:

Vague   The size of his hands made his smallness real. [How big were his hands? How small was he?]

Exact   Not until I saw his white, doll-like hands did I realize that he stood a full head shorter than most other men.

7c. Idioms

Idioms are expressions in any language that do not fit the rules for meaning or grammar—for instance, *put up with, plug away at, make off with.*

Because they are not governed by rules, idioms usually cause particular difficulty for people learning to speak and write a new language. But even native speakers of English misuse some idioms involving prepositions,° such as *agree on a plan, agree to a proposal,* and *agree with a person* or *charge for a purchase* and *charge with a crime.*

When in doubt about an idiom, consult your dictionary under the main word (*agree* and *charge* in the examples). (See also pp. 53–54 on verbs with particles.)

8

7d. Trite expressions

Trite expressions, or *clichés*, are phrases so old and so often repeated that they have become stale. Examples include *better late than never, beyond the shadow of a doubt, face the music, green with envy, ladder of success, point with pride, sneaking suspicion,* and *wise as an owl.*

Clichés may slide into your drafts. In editing, be wary of any expression you have heard or used before. Substitute fresh words of your own, or restate the idea in plain language.

8 Conciseness

Concise writing makes every word count. Conciseness is not the same as mere brevity: detail and originality should not be cut with needless words. Rather, the length of an expression should be appropriate to the thought.

You may find yourself writing wordily when you are unsure of your subject or when your thoughts are tangled. It's fine, even necessary, to stumble and grope while drafting. But you should straighten out your ideas and eliminate wordiness during revision and editing.

(8a.) Focusing on the subject and verb

The heart of every sentence is its subject,° which names who or what the sentence is about, and its verb,° which specifies what the subject does or is. When the subject and verb do not identify the key actor and action, the sentence is bound to be wordy. In the examples below, the subjects and verbs are italicized.

Wordy	The *occurrence* of the winter solstice, the shortest day of the year, *is* an event occurring about December 22.
Revised	The winter *solstice,* the shortest day of the year, *occurs* about December 22.

Focusing on the subject and verb can help you with most of the editing techniques discussed below.

(8b.) Cutting empty words

Cutting words that contribute nothing to your meaning will make your writing move faster and work harder.

Wordy	As far as I am concerned, because of the fact that a situation of discrimination continues to exist in the field of medicine, women have not at the present time achieved equality with men.
Concise	Because of continuing discrimination in medicine, women have not yet achieved equality with men.

Some empty expressions can be cut entirely, such as *all things considered, a person by the name of, as far as I'm concerned, for all intents and purposes, in a manner of speaking,* and *more or less.* Others can also be cut, usually along with some of the words around them: *area, aspect, case, element, factor, field, kind, manner, nature, situation, thing, type.* Still others can be reduced from several words to a single word—for instance, *at the present time* and *in today's society* both reduce to *now.*

(8c.) Cutting unneeded repetition

Unnecessary repetition weakens sentences and paragraphs.

8c

Wordy   Many unskilled workers *without training in a particular job* are unemployed *and do not have any work.* These *unskilled workers* depend on government aid.

Concise   Many unskilled workers are unemployed. *They* depend on government aid.

Be especially alert to phrases that say the same thing twice. In the following examples, only the underlined words are needed: <u>circle</u> around, <u>consensus</u> of opinion, <u>cooperate</u> together, dead <u>body</u>, final <u>completion</u>, <u>the future</u> to come, important (basic) <u>essentials</u>, <u>repeat</u> again, <u>return</u> again, <u>square (round)</u> in shape, surrounding <u>circumstances</u>.

(8d.)   Reducing clauses and phrases

Modifiers° can be expanded or contracted depending on the emphasis you want to achieve. (Generally, the longer a construction, the more emphasis it has.) When editing your sentences, consider whether any modifiers can be reduced without loss of emphasis or clarity.

Wordy   The Channel Tunnel, *which links Britain and France,* bores through *a bed of solid chalk that is forty kilometres across.*

Revised   The Channel Tunnel *linking Britain and France* bores through *forty kilometres of solid chalk.*

(8e.)   Using strong verbs

Weak verbs such as *is, has,* and *make* stall sentences and usually carry the extra baggage of unneeded or vague words.

Wordy   The drillers *made slow advancement,* and costs *were over* $5 million a day. The slow progress *was worrisome for* backers, who *had had expectations of* high profits.

Concise   The drillers *advanced slowly,* and costs *topped* $5 million a day. The slow progress *worried* backers, who *had expected* high profits.

8f. Using the active voice

In the verb's active voice,° the verb's subject names the performer of the verb's action (*banks* <u>*invested*</u>). In the passive voice,° in contrast, the verb's subject names the receiver of the verb's action (*funds* <u>*were invested*</u>). (See pp. 48–49 for more on the construction of the active and passive voice.)

The active voice is usually clearer and more concise than the passive voice. Reserve the passive voice mainly for emphasizing the receiver rather than the performer of the verb's action.

Wordy passive Up to *five metres* of chalk an hour *were devoured* by the drill.

Concise active The *drill devoured* up to five metres of chalk an hour.

8g. Cutting *there is* or *it is*

Sentences beginning *there is* or *it is* (called expletive constructions°) are sometimes useful to emphasize a change in direction, but usually they just add needless words.

Wordy *There are more than half a million share-holders who* have invested in the tunnel. *It is they and the banks that* hope to profit now that the tunnel is open.

Concise *More than half a million shareholders* have invested in the tunnel. *They and the banks* hope to profit now that the tunnel is open.

8h. Combining sentences

Often the information in two or more sentences can be combined into one tight sentence.

Wordy So far, business has been disappointing. Fewer travellers than were expected have boarded the tunnel train. The train runs between London and Paris.

Revised So far, business has been disappointing, with fewer travellers than expected boarding the tunnel train between London and Paris.

8h

III Sentence Parts and Patterns

Checklist for Sentence Parts and Patterns

This checklist focuses on the most common and potentially confusing grammatical errors.

✓ Verbs

Have you used the correct forms of irregular verbs such as *has <u>broken</u>* [not *has <u>broke</u>*]? (See opposite.) Have you used helping verbs where required, as in *she has been* [not *she <u>been</u>*]? (See p. 40.) Have you matched verbs to their subjects, as in *The list of items is* [not *are*] *long*? (See p. 49.)

✓ Pronouns

Do pronouns match the words they refer to, as in *Each of the women had <u>her</u>* [not *their*] *say*? (See p. 158.) Do pronouns refer clearly to the words they substitute for, avoiding uncertainties such as *Jill thanked Tracy when <u>she</u>* [Jill or Tracy?] *arrived*? (See p. 60.) Are pronouns consistent, avoiding shifts such as *When one enters college, you meet new ideas*? (See p. 62.)

✓ Modifiers

Do modifiers fall close to the words they describe, as in *Trash cans <u>without lids</u> invite animals* [not *Trash cans invite animals <u>without lids</u>*]? (See p. 67.) Do modifiers clearly modify another word in the sentence, as in *<u>Jogging, she</u> pulled a muscle* [not *<u>Jogging, a muscle was pulled</u>*]? (See p. 69.)

✓ Sentence faults

Are your sentences complete, each with a subject and a verb and none a free-standing subordinate clause? For instance, *But first <u>she</u> called the police* [not *But first called the police*]; *New stores <u>open</u> weekly* [not *New stores weekly*]; and *The new cow calved after the others did* [not *The new cow calved. <u>After the others did</u>*]? (See p. 71.) Within a sentence, have you linked main clauses with a comma and a coordinating conjunction (*Cars jam the roadways, <u>and</u> they contribute to smog*), with a semicolon (*Many parents did not attend; they did not want to get involved*), or with a semicolon and a conjunctive adverb (*The snow fell heavily; <u>however</u>, it soon melted*)? (See p. 73.)

Verbs

9 Verb Forms

Verb forms may give you trouble when the verb is irregular, when you omit certain endings, or when you need to use helping verbs.

***Sing/sang/sung* and other irregular verbs**

Most verbs are REGULAR: their past-tense form° and past participle° end in *-d* or *-ed*:

Today the birds *migrate*. They *soar*. [Plain form° of verb.]

Yesterday the birds *migrated*. They *soared*. [Past-tense form.]

In the past the birds have *migrated*. They have *soared*. [Past participle.]

About two hundred IRREGULAR VERBS° in English create their past-tense form and past participle in some way besides adding *-d* or *-ed*. These irregular verbs include *become* (*became/become*), *begin* (*began/begun*), *give* (*gave/given*), and *sing* (*sang/sung*).

Today the birds *fly*. They *begin* migration. [Plain form.]

Yesterday the birds *flew*. They *began* migration. [Past-tense form.]

In the past the birds have *flown*. They have *begun* migration. [Past participle.]

Check a dictionary under a verb's plain form if you have any doubt about the verb's other forms. If the verb is regular, the dictionary will follow the plain form with the *-d* or *-ed* form. If the verb is irregular, the dictionary will follow the plain form with the past-tense form and then the past participle. If the dictionary gives only one irregular form after the plain form, the past-tense form and past participle are the same (*think, thought, thought*).

9b.   *-s* and *-ed* verb endings

Speakers of some English dialects and non-native speakers of English sometimes omit verb endings that are required by standard English. One is the *-s* ending on the verb when the subject° is *he, she, it,* or a singular noun° and the verb's action occurs in the present.

The letter *asks* (not *ask*) for a quick response.
The company *has* (not *have*) delayed responding.
The treasurer *doesn't* (not *don't*) have the needed data.

Delay *is* (not *be*) costly.

A second omitted ending is the *-d* or *-ed* needed when (1) the verb's action occurred in the past (*we bagged*), (2) the verb form functions as a modifier° (*used cars*), or (3) the verb form combines with a form of *be* or *have* (*was supposed, has asked*).

The company *used to* (not *use to*) be more responsive.
We *provided* (not *provide*) the *requested* (not *request*) data as soon as we were *asked* (not *ask*).
We were *supposed* (not *suppose*) to be the best in the industry.

9c.   Helping verbs + main verbs ESL

Helping verbs° combine with main verbs° in specific ways.

Form of *be* + present participle

Create the progressive tenses° with *be, am, is, are, was, were,* or *been* followed by the main verb's present participle° (ending in *-ing*).

She *is working* on a new book.

Be and *been* require additional helping verbs to form progressive tenses.

can	might	should	}		have	}	
could	must	will	*be* working	has	*been* working
may	shall	would	}		had	}	

When forming the progressive tenses, be sure to use the *-ing* form of the main verb.

Note Verbs that express mental states or activities rather than physical actions do not usually appear in the progressive tenses. These verbs include *adore, appear,* *believe, belong, have, hear, know, like, love, need, see, taste, think, understand,* and *want.*

Faulty	She *is wanting* to understand contemporary ethics.
Revised	She *wants* to understand contemporary ethics.

Form of *be* + past participle

Create the passive voice° with *be, am, is, are, was, were, being,* or *been* followed by the main verb's past participle° (usually ending in -*d* or -*ed* or, for irregular verbs, in -*t* or -*n*).

Her latest book *was completed* in four months.

It *was brought* to the Premier's attention.

Be, being, and *been* require additional helping verbs to form the passive voice.

have ⎫
has ⎬ *been* completed
had ⎭

am ⎫ was
is ⎬ were ⎫ *being* completed
are ⎭

will *be* completed

Be sure to use the main verb's past participle for the passive voice.

Note Use only transitive verbs° to form the passive voice.

Faulty	A philosophy conference *was occurred* that week. [*Occur* is not a transitive verb.]
Revised	A philosophy conference *occurred* that week.

Form of *have* + past participle

Four forms of *have* serve as helping verbs: *have, has, had, having.* One of these forms plus the main verb's past participle creates one of the perfect tenses.°

Some students *have complained* about the laboratory.

Others *had complained* before.

Will and other helping verbs sometimes accompany forms of *have* in the perfect tenses.

Several more students *will have complained* by the end of the week.

Form of *do* + plain form

Always with the plain form° of the main verb, three forms of *do* serve as helping verbs: *do, does, did.* These forms have three uses:

- To pose a question: *How <u>did</u> the trial <u>end</u>?*
- To emphasize the main verb: *It <u>did end</u> eventually.*
- To negate the main verb, along with *not* or *never: The judge <u>did not withdraw</u>.*

Be sure to use the main verb's plain form with any form of *do*.

Faulty   The judge did *remained* in court.

Revised The judge did *remain* in court.

Modal + plain form

The MODALS are 10 helping verbs that never change form.

can	may	must	shall	will
could	might	ought	should	would

The modals indicate necessity, obligation, permission, possibility, and other meanings. They are always used with the plain form of the main verb.

Most of the students *can speak* English, but they *may struggle* on written tests. *Will* the scores *reflect* their knowledge?

10 Verb Tenses

Definitions and examples of the verb tenses appear on pp. 208–209. The following are the most common trouble spots.

(10a.) Uses of the present tense (*sing*)

Most academic and business writing uses the past tense° (*the rebellion <u>occurred</u>*), but the present tense has several distinctive uses:

Action occurring now
We *define* the problem differently.

Habitual or recurring action
Banks regularly *undergo* audits.

A general truth
The earth *is* round.

Discussion of literature, film, and so on
Huckleberry Finn *has* adventures we all envy.

Future time
Funding *ends* in less than a year.

 Uses of the perfect tenses
(*have/had/will have sung*)

The perfect tenses° generally indicate an action completed before another specific time or action. The present perfect tense° also indicates action begun in the past and continued into the present.

present perfect
The dancer *has performed* here only once.

present perfect
Critics *have written* about the performance ever since.

past perfect
The dancer *had trained* in Asia before his performance here 10 years ago.

future perfect
He *will have performed* here again by next month.

10c

(10c.) **Consistency in tense**

Within a sentence, the tenses of verbs and verb forms need not be identical as long as they reflect actual changes in time: *Our children will enjoy the trees we planted that summer after we bought the house.* But needless shifts in tense will confuse or distract readers.

Inconsistent   After weeks of preparation, the Canadian Corps *attacked* the German trenches at Vimy Ridge during Easter 1917. The Canadian troops, who *fight* together for the first time at Vimy, *lose* over 10,000 men in the battle.

Revised   After weeks of preparation, the Canadian Corps *attacked* the German trenches at Vimy Ridge during Easter 1917. The Canadian troops, who *fought* together for the first time at Vimy, *lost* over 10,000 men in the battle.

(10d.) Sequence of tenses

The SEQUENCE OF TENSES is the relation between the verb tense in a main clause° and the verb tense in a subordinate clause.°

Past or past perfect tense in main clause

When the verb in the main clause is in the past tense° or past perfect tense,° the verb in the subordinate clause must also be past or past perfect.

> The researchers *discovered* [past] that people *varied* [past] widely in their knowledge of public events.

> The variation *occurred* [past] because respondents *had been born* [past perfect] in different decades.

> None of them *had been born* [past perfect] when Sir Robert Borden *was* [past] prime minister.

Exception Always use the present tense° for a general truth, such as *The earth is round.*

> Few *understood* [past] that popular prime ministers *are* [present] not necessarily good prime ministers.

Conditional sentences ESL

A CONDITIONAL SENTENCE usually consists of a subordinate clause beginning *if, when,* or *unless* and a main clause stating the result. The three kinds of conditional sentences use distinctive verbs.
• For factual statements that something always or usually happens whenever something else happens, use the present tense in both clauses.

> When a voter *casts* [present] a ballot, he or she *has* [present] complete privacy.

If the linked events occurred in the past, use the past tense in both clauses.

> The youngest candidate *won* [past] even though she *received* [past] only 40 percent of the vote.

• For predictions, generally use the present tense in the subordinate clause and the future tense° in the main clause.

present   future
Unless her party *gains* more support, however, it *will lose* the next election.

- For speculations about events that are possible though unlikely, use the past tense in the subordinate clause and *would, could,* or *might* plus the verb's plain form in the main clause.

past
If women *had* more confidence in the system, they

would + verb
would run more often.

Use *were* instead of *was* when the subject is *I, he, she, it,* or a singular noun.

past   *would* + verb
If a woman candidate *were* more confident, she *would run* for office.

10d

For events that are impossible now—that are contrary to fact—use the same forms as above (including the distinctive *were* when applicable).

past   *might* + verb
If Nellie McClung *were* alive, she *might inspire* more women to run.

For events that were impossible in the past, use the past perfect tense in the subordinate clause and *would, could,* or *might* plus the present perfect tense° in the main clause.

past perfect
If Nellie McClung *had stood* for Parliament when

might + present perfect
young, she *might have become* prime minister one day.

The last four examples above illustrate the subjunctive mood of verbs. See Chapter 11.

Indirect quotations ESL

An indirect quotation° usually appears in a subordinate clause, and its verb depends on the verb in the main clause.

When the verb in the main clause is in the present tense, the verb in the indirect quotation (subordinate clause) is in the same tense as the original quotation.

present   present
McClung *writes* that it *is* not so much a woman's duty

present
to bring children into the world as it *is* to see what sort

present
of a world she *is* bringing them into. [Quotation: "It *is* not so much a woman's duty to bring children into the world as it *is* to see what sort of a world . . . she *is* bringing them into."]

When the verb in the main clause is in the past tense, the verb in the indirect quotation usually changes tense from the original quotation. Present tense changes to past tense.

past   past
McClung *wrote* that it *was* not so much a woman's duty
                          past
to bring children into the world as it *was* to see what
              past
sort of a world she *was* bringing them into. [Quotation: "It *is* not so much a woman's duty to bring children into the world as it *is* to see what sort of a world . . . she *is* bringing them into."]

Past tense and present perfect tense change to past perfect tense. (Past perfect tense does not change.)

past   past perfect
McClung *observed* that the pioneers *had trusted* in God. [Quotation: "They *trusted* in God. . . ."]

11 Verb Mood

The MOOD° of a verb indicates whether a sentence is a statement or a question (*The theatre <u>needs</u> help. <u>Can</u> you <u>help</u> the theatre?*), a command (*<u>Help</u> the theatre*), or a suggestion, desire, or other non-factual expression (*I wish I <u>were</u> an actor*).

(11a.) Consistency in mood

Shifts in mood within a sentence or among related sentences can be confusing. Such shifts occur most frequently in directions.

Inconsistent	Dissolve the crystals in the liquid. Then you should heat the solution to 120°C.
Revised	Dissolve the crystals in the liquid. Then *heat* the solution to 120°C.

(11b.) Subjunctive mood: *I wish I were*

The SUBJUNCTIVE MOOD° expresses a suggestion, requirement, or desire, or it states a condition that is
contrary to fact (that is, imaginary or hypothetical).

- Suggestion or requirement with the verb *ask, insist,
  urge, require, recommend,* or *suggest:* use the verb's
  plain form° with all subjects.

  Rules require that every donation *be* mailed.

- Desire or present condition contrary to fact: use the
  verb's past-tense form;° for *be,* use the past-tense
  form *were.*

  If the theatre *were* in better shape and *had* more money,
  its future would be guaranteed.
  I wish I *were* able to donate money.

- Past condition contrary to fact: use the verb's past-
  perfect form° (*had* + past participle).

  The theatre would be better funded if it *had been* better
  managed.

  Note In a sentence expressing a condition contrary
  to fact, the helping verb° *would* or *could* does not
  appear in the clause beginning *if.*

  Not Many people would have helped if they *would
          have* known.

  But Many people would have helped if they *had*
          known.

  Notice also that *have,* not *of,* follows *would* or *could:*
  would <u>have</u> (not *of*) helped.

12 Verb Voice

The VOICE° of a verb tells whether the subject° of the
sentence performs the action (ACTIVE VOICE°) or is acted
upon (PASSIVE VOICE°).

Active voice Commercial services *expand* partici-
                pation on the internet.

Passive voice Participation on the internet *is ex-
                panded* by commercial services.

(12a.) Consistency in voice

A shift in voice (and subject) from one sentence to another can be awkward or even confusing.

Inconsistent Commercial *services provide* fairly inexpensive internet access, and *navigation is made* easy by their software.

Revised Commercial services provide fairly inexpensive internet access, and their *software makes* navigation easy.

(12b.) Active voice vs. passive voice

The active voice always names the actor in a sentence (whoever performs the verb's action), whereas the passive voice puts the actor in a phrase after the verb or even omits the actor altogether. Thus, the active voice is usually more clear, direct, and concise than the passive voice.

Weak passive The *internet is used* for research by many scholars, and its *expansion* to the general public *has been criticized* by some.

Strong active Many *scholars use* the internet for research, and *some have criticized* its expansion to the general public.

The passive voice is useful in two situations: when the actor is unknown and when the actor is unimportant or less important than the object of the action.

The internet *was established* in 1969 by the U.S. Department of Defense. The network *has* now *been extended* internationally to governments, universities, foundations, corporations, and private individuals. [In the first sentence the writer wishes to stress the internet rather than the Department of Defense. In the second sentence the actor is unknown or too complicated to name.]

After the solution *had been cooled* to 10°C, the acid *was added*. [The person who cooled and added, perhaps the writer, is less important than the facts that the solution was cooled and acid was added. Passive sentences are common in scientific writing.]

13 Agreement of Subject and Verb

A subject° and its verb° should agree in number° (singular, plural) and person° (first, second, third).

Cape Breton *artists excel* at traditional Celtic music.
        subject verb

Ashley MacIsaac is a popular fiddler.
  subject   verb

13a. Words between subject and verb

A catalogue of courses and requirements often *baffles* (not *baffle*) students.

The requirements stated in the catalogue *are* (not *is*) unclear.

Phrases beginning with *as well as, together with, along with,* and *in addition to* do not change the number of the subject.

The president, as well as the deans, *has* (not *have*) agreed to revise the catalogue.

13b. Subjects with *and*

Frost and Roethke *were* American poets who died in the same year.

Note When *each* or *every* precedes the compound subject, the verb is usually singular.

Each man, woman, and child *has* a right to be heard.

13c. Subjects with *or* or *nor*

When parts of a subject are joined by *or* or *nor*, the verb agrees with the nearer part.

Either the painter or the carpenter *knows* the cost.

The cabinet or the bookcases *are* too costly.

When one part of the subject is singular and the other is plural, the sentence will be awkward unless you put the plural part second.

Awkward Neither the owners nor the contractor *agrees*.

Improved Neither the contractor nor the owners *agree*.

(13d.) *Everyone* and other indefinite pronouns

Indefinite pronouns° such as *everyone, no one,* and *somebody* are usually singular in meaning, and they take singular verbs.

Something *smells*.   Neither *is* right.

A few indefinite pronouns such as *all, any, none,* and *some* may take a singular or plural verb depending on meaning.

All of the money *is* reserved for emergencies.

All of the funds *are* reserved for emergencies.

(13e.) *Team* and other collective nouns

A collective noun° such as *team* or *family* takes a singular verb when the group acts as a unit.

The group *agrees* that action is necessary.

But when the group's members act separately, use a plural verb.

The old group *have* gone their separate ways.

(13f.) *Who, which,* and *that*

When used as subjects, *who, which,* and *that* refer to another word in the sentence. The verb agrees with this other word.

13f

Mayor Garber ought to listen to the people who *work* for her.

Bardini is the only aide who *has* her ear.

Bardini is one of the aides who *work* unpaid. [Of the aides who work unpaid, Bardini is one.]

Bardini is the only one of the aides who *knows* the community. [Of the aides, only one, Bardini, knows the community.]

13g. *News* and other singular nouns ending in *-s*

Singular nouns° ending in *-s* include *athletics, economics, mathematics, news, physics, politics,* and *statistics.*

After so long a wait, the news *has* to be good.

Statistics *is* required of psychology majors.

These words take plural verbs when they describe individual items rather than whole bodies of activity or knowledge.

The statistics *prove* him wrong.

13h. Inverted word order

Is voting a right or a privilege?

Are a right and a privilege the same thing?

There *are* differences between them.

13i. *Is, are,* and other linking verbs

Make a linking verb° agree with its subject, usually the first element in the sentence, rather than with other words referring to the subject.

The child's sole support *is* her court-appointed guardians.

Her court-appointed guardians *are* the child's sole support.

14 Other Complications with Verbs ESL

Verbs often combine with other words in idioms° that must be memorized.

14a. Verb + gerund or infinitive

14a

A GERUND° is the -*ing* form of a verb used as a noun (*Smoking* kills). An INFINITIVE° is the plain form° of the verb plus *to* (*Try to quit*). Gerunds and infinitives may follow certain verbs but not others. And sometimes the use of a gerund or infinitive with the same verb changes the meaning of the verb.

Either gerund or infinitive

A gerund or an infinitive may follow these verbs with no significant difference in meaning: *begin, continue, hate, like, love, start*.

The pump began *working*. The pump began *to work*.

Meaning change with gerund or infinitive

With four verbs—*forget, remember, stop*, and *try*—a gerund has quite a different meaning from an infinitive.

The engineer stopped *watching* the pump. [She no longer watched.]

The engineer stopped *to watch* the pump. [She stopped in order to watch.]

Gerund, not infinitive

Do not use an infinitive after these verbs: *admit, adore, appreciate, avoid, deny, detest, discuss, enjoy, escape, finish, imagine, miss, practise, put off, quit, recall, resist, risk, suggest, tolerate*.

Faulty She suggested *to check* the pump.

Revised She suggested *checking* the pump.

Infinitive, not gerund

Do not use a gerund after these verbs: *agree, ask, assent, beg, claim, decide, expect, have, hope, manage, mean, offer, plan, pretend, promise, refuse, say, wait, want, wish.*

Faulty   She decided *checking* the pump.

Revised   She decided *to check* the pump.

Noun or pronoun + infinitive

The verbs *ask, expect, need, want,* and *would like* may be followed by an infinitive alone or by a noun° or pronoun° and an infinitive. A noun or pronoun changes the meaning.

She expected *to watch.*

She expected *her workers to watch.*

Some verbs *must* be followed by a noun or pronoun before an infinitive: *admonish, advise, allow, cause, command, convince, encourage, instruct, order, persuade, remind, require, tell, warn.*

She instructed *her workers to watch.*

Do not use *to* before the infinitive when it comes after one of the following verbs and a noun or pronoun: *feel, have, hear, let, make* ("force"), *see, watch.*

She let her workers *learn* by observation.

14b

(14b.) Verb + particle

Some verbs consist of two words: the verb itself and a PARTICLE°, a preposition° or adverb° that affects the meaning of the verb, as in *Look up the answer* (research the answer) or *Look over the answer* (check the answer). Many of these two-word verbs are defined in dictionaries. (There are some three-word verbs, too, such as *put up with* and *run out of.*)

Some two-word verbs may be separated in a sentence; others may not.

Inseparable two-word verbs

Verbs and particles that may not be separated by any other words include the following: *catch on, get along, give in, go out, grow up, keep on, look into, run into, run out of, speak up, stay away, take care of.*

| **Faulty** | Children *grow* quickly *up*. |
| **Revised** | Children *grow up* quickly. |

Separable two-word verbs

Most two-word verbs that take direct objects° may be separated by the object.

Parents *help out* their children.

Parents *help* their children *out*.

If the direct object is a pronoun,° the pronoun *must* separate the verb from the particle.

| **Faulty** | Parents *help out* them. |
| **Revised** | Parents *help* them *out*. |

The separable two-word verbs include the following: *call off, call up, fill out, fill up, give away, give back, hand in, help out, look over, look up, pick up, point out, put away, put back, put off, take out, take over, try on, try out, turn down.*

14b

Pronouns

15 Pronoun Forms

A noun° or pronoun° changes form to show the reader how it functions in a sentence. These forms—called CASES—are SUBJECTIVE° (such as *I, she, they, man*), OBJECTIVE° (such as *me, her, them, man*), and POSSESSIVE° (such as *my, her, their, man's*). A list of the case forms appears on pp. 198–199.

15b

15a. Compound subjects and objects: *she and I* vs. *her and me*

Subjects° and objects° consisting of two or more nouns and pronouns have the same case forms as they would if one pronoun stood alone.

compound subject
She and Steven discussed the proposal.

compound object
The proposal disappointed *her and him.*

To test for the correct form, try one pronoun alone in the sentence. The case form that sounds correct is probably correct for all parts of the compound.

The prize went to (*he, him*) and (*I, me*).

The prize went to *him.*

The prize went to *him and me.*

15b. Subject complements: *it was she*

Both a subject and a subject complement° appear in the same form—the subjective case.

subject
complement
The one who cares most is *she.*

If this construction sounds stilted to you, use the more natural order: <u>*She*</u> *is the one who cares most.*

(15c.) *Who* vs. *whom*

The choice between *who* and *whom* depends on the use of the word.

Questions

At the beginning of a question use *who* for a subject and *whom* for an object.

subject↘   object↙
Who wrote the policy?   *Whom* does it affect?

Test for the correct form by answering the question with the form of *he* or *she* that sounds correct. Then use the same form in the question.

(*Who, Whom*) does one ask?

One asks *her.*

Whom does one ask?

Subordinate clauses

In subordinate clauses° use *who* and *whoever* for all subjects, *whom* and *whomever* for all objects.

subject ↘
Give old clothes to *whoever* needs them.

object ↙
I don't know *whom* the mayor appointed.

Test for the correct form by rewriting the subordinate clause as a sentence. Replace *who* or *whom* with the form of *he* or *she* that sounds correct. Then use the same form in the original subordinate clause.

Few people know (*who, whom*) they should ask.

They should ask *her.*

Few people know *whom* they should ask.

Note Don't let expressions such as *I think* and *she says* confuse you when they come between the subject *who* and its verb.

subject ↘
He is the one *who* I think is best qualified.

(15d.) Other constructions

We or *us* with a noun

The choice of *we* or *us* before a noun depends on the use of the noun.

object of
preposition

Freezing weather is welcomed by *us* skaters.

subject

We skaters welcome freezing weather.

Pronoun in an appositive

An APPOSITIVE° is a word or word group that renames a noun or pronoun. Within an appositive the form of a pronoun depends on the function of the word the appositive renames.

object of verb

The class elected two representatives, Samir and *me*.

subject

Two representatives, Samir and *I*, were elected.

Pronoun after *than* or *as*

After *than* or *as* in a comparison, the form of a pronoun indicates what words may have been omitted. A subjective pronoun must be the subject of the omitted verb:

subject

Some critics like Glass more than *she* (does).

An objective pronoun must be the object of the omitted verb:

object

Some critics like Glass more than (they like) *her*.

Subject and object of an infinitive

An INFINITIVE° is the plain form° of the verb plus *to* (*to swim*). Both its object and its subject are in the objective form.

subject of
infinitive

The school asked *him* to speak.

object of
infinitive

Students chose to invite *him*.

Form before a gerund

A GERUND° is the *-ing* form of a verb used as a noun (*a runner's breathing*). Generally, use the possessive form of a pronoun or noun immediately before a gerund.

The coach disapproved of *their* lifting weights.

The *coach's* disapproving was a surprise.

15d

16 Agreement of Pronoun and Antecedent

The ANTECEDENT° of a pronoun° is the noun° or other pronoun it refers to.

Homeowners fret over *their* tax bills.
  antecedent   pronoun

Its amount makes the tax *bill* a dreaded document.
pronoun   antecedent

For clarity, a pronoun should agree with its antecedent in person° (first, second, third), number° (singular, plural), and gender° (masculine, feminine, neuter).

16b

16a. Antecedents with *and*

The dean and my adviser have offered *their* help.

Note When *each* or *every* precedes the compound antecedent, the pronoun is singular.

Every girl and woman took *her* seat.

16b. Antecedents with *or* or *nor*

When parts of an antecedent are joined by *or* or *nor*, the pronoun agrees with the nearer part.

Tenants or owners must present *their* grievances.

Either the tenant or the owner will have *her* way.

When one subject is plural and the other singular, put the plural subject second to avoid awkwardness.

Awkward   Neither the tenants nor the owner has yet made *her* case.

Revised   Neither the owner nor the tenants have yet made *their* case.

(16c.) *Everyone* and other indefinite pronouns

Most indefinite pronouns,° such as *anybody* and *everyone,* are singular in meaning. When they serve as antecedents to other pronouns, the other pronouns are also singular.

Everyone on the team had *her* own locker.

Each of the boys likes *his* teacher.

Note Tradition has called for *he* to refer to indefinite pronouns and other indefinite words (*child, adult, individual, person*), even when both masculine and feminine genders are intended. But increasingly this so-called generic (or generalized) *he* is considered inaccurate or unfair because it excludes females. To avoid it, try one of the following techniques.

Generic *he* Nobody in the class had the credits *he* needed.

• Substitute *he or she.*

Revised Nobody in the class had the credits *he or she* needed.

To avoid awkwardness, don't use *he or she* more than once in several sentences.

• Recast the sentence using a plural antecedent and pronoun.

Revised *All the students* in the class lacked the credits *they* needed.

• Rewrite the sentence to avoid the pronoun.

Revised Nobody in the class had the *needed credits.*

16d

(16d.) *Team* and other collective nouns

Use a singular pronoun with *team, family, group,* or another collective noun° when referring to the group as a unit.

The committee voted to disband *itself.*

When referring to the individual members of the group, use a plural pronoun.

The old group have gone *their* separate ways.

17 Reference of Pronoun to Antecedent

If a pronoun° does not refer clearly to the word it substitutes for (its ANTECEDENT), readers will have difficulty grasping the pronoun's meaning.

17b

17a.) Single antecedent

When either of two words can be a pronoun's antecedent, the reference will not be clear.

Confusing   The workers removed all the furniture from the room and cleaned *it.*

Revise such a sentence in one of two ways:

• Replace the pronoun with the appropriate noun.

Clear   The workers removed all the furniture from the room and cleaned *the room* (or *the furniture*).

• Avoid repetition by rewriting the sentence with the pronoun but with only one possible antecedent.

Clear   After removing all the furniture from *it*, the workers cleaned the room.

Clear   The workers cleaned all the furniture after removing *it* from the room.

17b.) Close antecedent

A clause° beginning *who, which,* or *that* should generally fall immediately after the word it refers to.

| Confusing | Jody found a dress in the attic *that* her aunt had worn. |
| Clear | In the attic Jody found a dress *that* her aunt had worn. |

(17c.) Specific antecedent

A pronoun should refer to a specific noun° or other pronoun.

Vague *this, that, which,* or *it*

This, that, which, or *it* should refer to a specific noun, not to a whole word group expressing an idea or situation.

| Confusing | Lord Selkirk's attempt to establish the Red River Colony was opposed by the fur traders of the North West Company and their Métis allies, who attacked. *This* led Selkirk to fight both on the battlefield and in the courts. |
| Clear | Lord Selkirk's attempt to establish the Red River Colony was opposed by the fur traders of the North West Company and their Métis allies, who attacked. *This opposition* led Selkirk to fight both on the battlefield and in the courts. |

Implied nouns

A pronoun cannot refer clearly to a noun that is merely implied by some other word or phrase, such as *news* in *newspaper* or *happiness* in *happy.*

Confusing	In Joan Cohen's advice *she* was not specific.
Clear	*Joan Cohen's advice* was not specific.
Confusing	She spoke once before, but *it* was sparsely attended.
Clear	She spoke once before, but *the speech* was sparsely attended.

17c

Indefinite *it* and *they*

It and *they* should have definite antecedents.

Confusing	In the average television drama *they* present a false picture of life.
Clear	The average television *drama* presents a false picture of life.

(17d.) Consistency in pronouns

Within a sentence or a group of related sentences, pronouns should be consistent.

Inconsistent	*One* finds when reading that *your* concentration improves with practice, so that *I* now comprehend more in less time.
Revised	*I* find when reading that *my* concentration improves with practice, so that I now comprehend more in less time.

17d

Modifiers

18 Adjectives and Adverbs

ADJECTIVES modify nouns° (_good_ child) and pronouns° (_special_ someone). ADVERBS modify verbs° (_see well_), adjectives (_very_ happy), other adverbs (_not_ very), and whole word groups (_Otherwise_, the room was empty). The only way to tell if a modifier should be an adjective or an adverb is to determine its function in the sentence.

18a. Adjective vs. adverb

18c

Use only adverbs, not adjectives, to modify verbs, adverbs, or other adjectives.

Not They took each other _serious_. They related _good_.

But They took each other _seriously_. They related _well_.

18b. Adjective with linking verb: _felt bad_

A modifier after a verb should be an adjective if it describes the subject,° an adverb if it describes the verb. In the first example below, the linking verb° _felt_ connects the subject and an adjective describing the subject.

The sailors felt _bad_.
  linking adjective
  verb

Some sailors fare _badly_ in rough weather.
  verb adverb

Good and _well_ are frequently confused after verbs.

Decker trained _well_. [Adverb.]

She felt _well_. Her prospects were _good_. [Adjectives.]

18c. Comparison of adjectives and adverbs

Comparison° allows adjectives and adverbs to show degrees of quality or amount by changing form: _red_, *redder, reddest; awful, more awful, most awful; quickly, less quickly, least quickly.* A dictionary will list the *-er* and *-est* endings if they can be used. Otherwise, use *more* and *most* or *less* and *least.*

Some modifiers are irregular, changing their spelling for comparison: for example, *good, better, best; many, more, most; badly, worse, worst.*

Comparing two or more than two

Use the *-er* form, *more,* or *less* when comparing two items. Use the *-est* form, *most,* or *least* when comparing three or more items.

> Of the two tests, the litmus is *better.*
> Of all six tests, the litmus is *best.*

Double comparisons

A double comparison combines the *-er* or *-est* ending with the word *more* or *most.* It is redundant.

> Chang was the *wisest* (not *most wisest*) person in town.
> He was *smarter* (not *more smarter*) than anyone else.

Complete comparisons

A comparison should be complete.

• The comparison should state a relation fully enough to ensure clarity.

Unclear Car makers worry about their industry more than environmentalists.

Clear Car makers worry about their industry more than environmentalists *do.*

Clear Car makers worry about their industry more than *they worry about* environmentalists.

• The items being compared should in fact be comparable.

Illogical The cost of an electric car is greater than a gasoline-powered car. [Illogically compares a cost and a car.]

Revised The cost of an electric car is greater than *the cost of* (or *that of*) a gasoline-powered car.

(18d.) **Double negatives**

A DOUBLE NEGATIVE° is a non-standard construction in which two negative words cancel each other out. For instance, *Jenny did <u>not</u> feel <u>nothing</u>* asserts that Jenny felt other than nothing, or something.

Faulty   Revenue Canada *cannot hardly* audit all tax returns. *None* of its audits *never* touch many cheaters.

Revised   Revenue Canada *cannot* audit all tax returns. Its audits *never* touch many cheaters.

(18e.)   ## Present and past participles as adjectives [ESL]

Both present participles° and past participles° may serve as adjectives: *a <u>burning</u> house, a <u>burned</u> house.* As in the examples, the two participles usually differ in the time they indicate.

But some present and past participles—those derived from verbs expressing feeling—can have altogether different meanings. The present participle refers to something that causes the feeling: *That was a <u>frightening</u> storm.* The past participle refers to something that experiences the feeling: *They quieted the <u>frightened</u> horses.* Similar pairs include the following: *annoying/annoyed, boring/bored, confusing/confused, exciting/excited, exhausting/exhausted, interesting/interested, pleasing/pleased, satisfying/satisfied, surprising/surprised, tiring/tired, troubling/troubled, worrying/worried.*

18f

(18f.)   ## Articles: *a, an, the* [ESL]

Articles° usually trouble native English speakers only in the choice of *a* versus *an: a* for words beginning with consonant sounds (*<u>a</u> bridge, <u>a</u> uniform*), *an* for words beginning with vowel sounds, including silent *h*'s (*<u>an</u> apple, <u>an</u> urge, <u>an</u> hour*).

For non-native speakers, *a, an,* and *the* can be difficult, because many other languages use such words quite differently or not at all. In English, their uses depend on the kinds of nouns they precede and the context they appear in.

Singular count nouns

A COUNT NOUN° names something countable and can form a plural: *glass/glasses, mountain/mountains, child/children, woman/women.*

- *A* or *an* precedes a singular count noun when your reader does not already know its identity, usually because you have not mentioned it before.

A scientist in our chemistry department developed *a* process to strengthen metals. [*Scientist* and *process* are being introduced for the first time.]

- *The* precedes a singular count noun that has a specific identity for your reader, usually because (1) you have mentioned it before, (2) you identify it immediately before or after you state it, (3) it is unique (the only one in existence), or (4) it refers to an institution or facility that is shared by the community.

A scientist in our chemistry department developed a process to strengthen metals. *The* scientist patented *the* process. [*Scientist* and *process* were identified in the preceding sentence.]

The most productive laboratory is *the* research centre in the chemistry department. [*Most productive* identifies *laboratory*, and *in the chemistry department* identifies *research centre*.]

The sun rises in *the* east. [*Sun* and *east* are unique.]

Some women now aspire to *the* priesthood. [*Priesthood* is a shared institution.]

Plural count nouns

A or *an* never precedes a plural noun. *The* does not precede a plural noun that names a general category. *The* does precede a plural noun that names specific representatives of a category.

Men and *women* are different. [*Men* and *women* name general categories.]

The women formed a team. [*Women* refers to specific people.]

Non-count nouns

A NON-COUNT NOUN° names something that is not usually considered countable in English and thus does not form a plural. Examples include *advice, cereal, confidence, equipment, evidence, furniture, health, honesty, information, knowledge, lumber, mail, oil, pollution, research, silver, truth, water, weather, work.*

A or *an* never precedes a non-count noun. *The* does precede a non-count noun that names specific representatives of a general category.

18f

Vegetation suffers from drought. [*Vegetation* names a general category.]

The vegetation in the park withered or died. [*Vegetation* refers to specific plants.]

Note Many nouns are sometimes count nouns and sometimes non-count nouns.

The library has *a room* for readers. [*Room* is a count noun meaning "walled area."]

The library has *room* for reading. [*Room* is a non-count noun meaning "space."]

Proper nouns

A PROPER NOUN° names a particular person, place, or thing and begins with a capital letter: *February, Joe Allen. A* or *an* never precedes a proper noun. *The* does only occasionally, as with oceans (*the Pacific*), regions (*the Middle East*), rivers (*the Fraser*), some countries (*the United States*), and some universities (*the University of Toronto*).

Ian lives in *Fredericton,* where he attends *the University of New Brunswick.*

19a

19 Misplaced and Dangling Modifiers

For clarity, modifiers generally must fall close to the words they modify.

19a. Misplaced modifiers

A MISPLACED MODIFIER° falls in the wrong place in a sentence. It may be awkward, confusing, or even unintentionally funny.

Clear placement

Confusing He served steak to the men *on paper plates.*

Revised He served the men steak *on paper plates.*

Confusing   Many dogs are killed by automobiles and
trucks *roaming unleashed.*

Revised   Many dogs *roaming unleashed* are killed
by automobiles and trucks.

Only and other limiting modifiers

LIMITING MODIFIERS include *almost, even, exactly,
hardly, just, merely, nearly, only, scarcely,* and *simply.*
They should fall immediately before the word or word
group they modify.

Unclear   They *only* saw each other during meals.

Revised   They saw *only* each other during meals.

Revised   They saw each other *only* during meals.

Infinitives and other grammatical units

Some grammatical units should generally not be split
by long modifiers. For example, a long modifier between
subject° and verb° can be awkward and confusing.

Awkward   The *wreckers,* soon after they began demolishing the old house, *discovered* a large box
of coins.

Revised   Soon after they began demolishing the
old house, the *wreckers discovered* a large
box of coins.

A SPLIT INFINITIVE°—a modifier placed between *to*
and the verb—can be especially awkward and annoys
many readers.

Awkward   Forecasters expected temperatures *to* not *rise.*

Revised   Forecasters expected temperatures not *to rise.*

A split infinitive may sometimes be unavoidable without rewriting, though it may still bother some readers.

Several industries expect *to* more than *triple* their use of
robots.

Order of adjectives ESL

English follows distinctive rules for arranging two or three adjectives before a noun. (A string of more than three adjectives before a noun is rare.) Adjectives always precede the noun except when they are subject complements,° and they follow this order:

1. Article or other word marking the noun: *a, an, the, this, Mary's*
2. Word of opinion: *beautiful, disgusting, important, fine*
3. Word about measurement: *small, huge, short, towering*
4. Word about shape: *round, flat, square, triangular*
5. Word about age: *old, young, new, ancient*
6. Word about colour: *green, white, black, magenta*
7. Word about origin (nationality, religion, etc.): *European, Iranian, Jewish, Parisian*
8. Word about material: *wooden, gold, nylon, stone*

Examples of this order include *a new provincial law, all recent business reports,* and *the blue litmus paper.*

19b

(19b.) Dangling modifiers

A DANGLING MODIFIER does not sensibly modify anything in its sentence.

Dangling *Passing the building,* the vandalism became visible.

Like most dangling modifiers, this one introduces a sentence, contains a verb form (*passing*), and implies but does not name a subject (whoever is passing). Readers assume that this implied subject is the same as the subject of the sentence (*vandalism*). When it is not, the modifier "dangles" unconnected to the rest of the sentence.

Revise dangling modifiers to achieve the emphasis you want.

- Rewrite the dangling modifier as a complete clause with its own stated subject and verb. Readers can accept different subjects when they are both stated.

Dangling *Passing the building,* the vandalism became visible.

Revised *As we passed* the building, the vandalism became visible.

- Change the subject of the sentence to a word the modifier properly describes.

Dangling   *Trying to understand the causes,* vandalism
has been extensively studied.

Revised   Trying to understand the causes, *researchers
have* extensively *studied* vandalism.

19b

Sentence Faults

20 Sentence Fragments

A SENTENCE FRAGMENT is part of a sentence that is set off as if it were a whole sentence by an initial capital letter and a final period or other end punctuation. It lacks one or both of the essential ingredients of a complete sentence: a subject and a verb. Although writers occasionally use fragments deliberately and effectively, readers perceive most fragments as serious errors in standard English. Use the tests below to ensure that you have linked or separated your ideas both appropriately for your meaning and correctly, without creating sentence fragments.

Note ESL Some languages other than English allow the omission of the subject° or the verb.° Except in commands (*Close the door*), English always requires you to state the subject and verb.

20a

20a. Tests for fragments

A word group punctuated as a sentence should pass *all three* of the following tests. If it does not, it is a fragment and needs to be revised.

Test 1: Find the verb.

The verb in a complete sentence can change form as on the left below. A verb form° that cannot change this way (as on the right) cannot serve as a sentence verb.

	Complete sentences	**Sentence fragments**
Singular	The baboon *looks*.	The baboon *looking*.
Plural	The baboons *look*.	The baboons *looking*.
Present	The baboon *looks*.	
Past	The baboon *looked*.	The baboon *looking*.
Future	The baboon *will look*.	

Test 2: Find the subject.

The subject of the sentence will usually come before the verb. If there is no subject, the word group is probably a fragment.

Fragment   And eyed the guard nervously.

Revised   And *he* eyed the guard nervously.

Test 3: Make sure the clause is not subordinate.

A SUBORDINATE CLAUSE° begins with either a subordinating conjunction° (such as *because, if, when*) or a relative pronoun° (*who, which, that*). Subordinate clauses serve as parts of sentences, not as whole sentences.

Fragment   When the next cage rattled.

Revised   The next cage rattled.

Note Questions beginning with *who, whom,* or *which* are not sentence fragments: *Who rattled the cage?*

(20b.)   Revision of fragments

Correct sentence fragments in one of two ways depending on the importance of the information in the fragment.

• As in all examples so far, rewrite the fragment as a complete sentence. The information in the fragment will then have the same importance as that in other complete sentences.
• Combine the fragment with the appropriate main clause. The information in the fragment will then be subordinated to that in the main clause.

Fragment   The challenger was a newcomer. *Who was unusually fierce.*

Revised   The challenger was a newcomer who was unusually fierce.

21 Comma Splices and Fused Sentences

When you combine two complete sentences (main clauses°) in one sentence, you need to give readers a clear signal that one clause is ending and the other beginning. In a COMMA SPLICE° two main clauses are joined (or spliced) only by a comma, which is usually too weak to signal the link between main clauses.

Comma splice   The ship was huge, its mast stood 80 feet high.

In a FUSED SENTENCE (or RUN-ON SENTENCE)° the clauses are not separated at all.

Fused sentence   The ship was huge its mast stood 80 feet high.

(21a.) Main clauses without *and, but, or, nor, for, so, yet*

And, but, or, or another coordinating conjunction° often signals the joining of main clauses. When a sentence with two main clauses lacks this signal (and is thus a comma splice or fused sentence), revise the sentence in one of the following ways:

- Insert a coordinating conjunction when the ideas in the main clauses are closely related and equally important.

  Comma splice   Some laboratory-grown foods taste good, they are nutritious.

  Revised   Some laboratory-grown foods taste good, *and* they are nutritious.

In a fused sentence insert a comma and a coordinating conjunction.

  Fused sentence   Chemists have made much progress they still have a way to go.

  Revised   Chemists have made much progress, *but* they still have a way to go.

- Insert a semicolon between clauses if the relation between the ideas is very close and obvious without a conjunction.

  Comma splice   Good taste is rare in laboratory-grown vegetables, they are usually bland.

  Revised   Good taste is rare in laboratory-grown vegetables; they are usually bland.

- Make the clauses into separate sentences when the ideas expressed are only loosely related.

  Comma splice   Chemistry has contributed to our understanding of foods, many foods such as wheat and beans can be produced in the laboratory.

21a

Revised   Chemistry has contributed to our understanding of foods. Many foods such as wheat and beans can be produced in the laboratory.

• Subordinate one clause to the other when one idea is less important than the other. The subordinate clause will modify something in the main clause.

Comma splice   The vitamins are adequate, the flavour and colour are deficient.

Revised   *Even though* the vitamins are adequate, the flavour and colour are deficient.

21b.   Main clauses related by *however, thus, for example,* and so on

21b

Two kinds of words can describe how one main clause relates to another: conjunctive adverbs,° such as *however, instead, meanwhile,* and *thus;* and other transitional expressions,° such as *even so, for example, in fact,* and *of course.* Two main clauses related by all conjunctive adverbs and most transitional expressions must be separated by a period or by a semicolon. The connecting word or phrase is also generally set off by a comma or commas.

Comma splice   Most Canadians know that they should engage in regular exercise, however they do not always do so.

Revised   Most Canadians know that they should engage in regular exercise. *However,* they do not always do so.

Revised   Most Canadians know that they should engage in regular exercise; *however,* they do not always do so.

Revised   Most Canadians know that they should engage in regular exercise; they do not, however, always do so.

To test whether a word or phrase is a conjunctive adverb or transitional expression, try repositioning it in its clause. It can move.

Most Canadians know that they should engage in regular exercise; they do not, *however,* always do so.

IV Punctuation

Punctuation Checklist

This checklist focuses on the most troublesome punctuation marks and uses, showing correctly punctuated sentences with brief explanations.

✓ Comma

Subways are convenient, <u>but</u> they are costly to build. Subways are convenient <u>but</u> costly. [With *and*, *but*, etc., only between main clauses. See p. 78.]

<u>Because</u> of their cost, new subways are rarely built. [With an introductory element. See pp. 78–79.]

Light rail, <u>which is less costly</u>, is often more feasible. Those <u>who favour mass transit</u> often propose light rail. [With a non-essential element, not with an essential element. See pp. 79–80.]

In a few older cities, commuters can choose from <u>subways, buses, light rail, and railroads</u>. [Separating items in a series. See pp. 80–81.]

✓ Semicolon

She chose carpentry; she wanted manual work. She had a law degree; <u>however</u>, she became a carpenter. [Between main clauses not joined by *and*, *but*, etc., and those joined by *however*, *for example*, etc. See pp. 82–83.]

✓ Colon

The school has one goal: to train businesspeople. [With a main clause to introduce information. See p. 84.]

✓ Apostrophe

Bill <u>Smith's</u> dog saved the life of the <u>Smiths'</u> grandchild. [Showing possession: with *-'s* for singular nouns; with *-'* only for plural nouns ending in *-s*. See pp. 85–86.]

<u>Its</u> [for <u>The dog's</u>] bark warned the family. <u>It's</u> [for <u>It is</u>] an intelligent dog. [Not with possessive pronouns, only with contractions. See pp. 86–87.]

22 End Punctuation

End a sentence with one of three punctuation marks:
a period, a question mark, or an exclamation point.

(22a.) Period for most sentences and some abbreviations

Statements

The airline went bankrupt.
It no longer flies.

Mild commands

Think of the possibilities.
See page 27.

Indirect questions°

The article asks how we can improve math education.
It asks what cost we are willing to pay.

Abbreviations

p.	Ph.D.	Mr.
Dr.	e.g.	Mrs.
St.	i.e.	Ms.

Periods may be omitted from abbreviations of two
or more words written in all-capital letters.

MD	BC	AM	IBM	CRTC
BA	AD	PM	CUSO	AIDS

Note When a sentence ends in an abbreviation with
a period, don't add a second period: *The university offers a well-respected Ph.D.*

(22b.) Question mark for direct questions°

What is the result?
What is the difference between those proposals?

(22c.) Exclamation point for strong statements and commands

No! We must not lose this election!
"Oh!" she gasped.

Note Use exclamation points sparingly, even in informal writing. They can make writing sound overly dramatic.

23 The Comma

The comma is the most common punctuation mark inside sentences. Its main uses (and misuses) appear below.

23a. Comma with *and, but, or, nor, for, so, yet*

Between main clauses

Use a comma before *and, but, or, nor, for, so,* and *yet* (the coordinating conjunctions°) when they link complete sentences (main clauses°).

Banks offer many services, *but* they could do more.

Many banks offer investment advice, *and* they help small businesses establish credit.

Note The comma goes before, not after, the coordinating conjunction.

Not between words, phrases, or subordinate clauses

Generally, do not use a comma before *and, but, or,* and *nor* when they link elements other than main clauses: words, phrases,° subordinate clauses.°

Not One bank *established* special accounts for older depositors, *and counselled* them on investments.

But One bank established special accounts for older depositors and counselled them on investments.

23b. Comma with introductory elements

Use a comma after most elements that begin sentences and are distinct from the main clause.

When a new century nears, futurists multiply.

Fortunately, some news is good.

You may omit the comma after a short introductory element if there's no risk that the reader will run the introductory element and main clause together: *By the year 2010 we may have reduced pollution.*

Note The subject° of a sentence is not an introductory element but a part of the main clause. Thus, do not use a comma to separate the subject and its verb.

Not   Some *pessimists, may be* disappointed.

But   Some pessimists may be disappointed.

(23c.) Comma or commas with interrupting and concluding elements

Use a comma or commas to set off elements that provide non-essential information—information that could be deleted without altering the basic meaning of the sentence or leaving it too general.

Note When non-essential information falls in the middle of the sentence, be sure to use one comma *before* and one *after* it.

Around non-restrictive elements

A NON-RESTRICTIVE ELEMENT° adds information about a word in the sentence but does not limit the word to a particular individual or group. Omitting the element may remove incidental details, but it does not affect the sentence's basic meaning.

> Hai Nguyen, *who emigrated from Vietnam*, lives in Edmonton.

> His company, *which is ten years old*, studies air and water pollution.

> Nguyen's family lives in Vancouver and Winnipeg, *even though he lives in Edmonton.*

Non-restrictive elements may be modifiers, like those above, or APPOSITIVES°, words or word groups that rename nouns.

> Nguyen's work, *advanced research into air pollution*, keeps him in Edmonton.

> His wife, *Tina Nguyen*, reports for a newspaper in Winnipeg.

Not around restrictive elements

Do not use commas to set off RESTRICTIVE ELEMENTS°, modifiers, and appositives containing information essential to the meaning of the sentence. Omitting a restrictive element alters the sentence's meaning substantially, leaving the sentence unclear or too general.

People *who join recycling programs* rarely complain about the extra work.

The programs *that succeed* are often staffed by volunteers.

The label *"Recycle"* on products becomes a command.

Most people recycle *because they believe they have a responsibility to the earth.*

Around absolute phrases

An ABSOLUTE PHRASE° consists usually of the *-ing* form of a verb plus a subject for the verb. The phrase modifies the whole main clause of the sentence.

Student loans, *their costs always rising*, are a concern for many students.

Around parenthetical expressions

A PARENTHETICAL EXPRESSION° is a supplemental or transitional word or phrase, such as *of course,* or *however,* or a brief example or fact. It can be enclosed in parentheses (see pp. 92–93) or, with more emphasis, in commas.

Many students, *it seems*, have no choice but to incur large debts.

Around phrases of contrast

Students may focus on their loan, *not their education*.

Around **yes** and **no**

Governments agree that, *yes*, students need financial assistance to pay for books and tuition.

Around words of direct address

Heed this lesson, *readers*.

(23d.) Commas with series

Between series items

Use commas to separate the items in lists, or series.

The names *Belial, Beelzebub, and Lucifer* sound ominous.

The comma before the last item in a series (before *and*) is actually optional, but it is never wrong and it is usually clearer.

Not around series

Do not use a comma *before* or *after* a series.

Not   The skills of, *agriculture, herding, and hunting,* sustained the First Nations.

But   The skills of agriculture, herding, and hunting sustained the First Nations.

(23e.) Comma with adjectives

Between equal adjectives

Use a comma between two or more adjectives° when each one modifies the same word equally. As a test, such adjectives could be joined by *and*.

The *dirty, dented* car was a neighbourhood eyesore.

Not between unequal adjectives

Do not use a comma between adjectives when one forms a unit with the modified word. As a test, the two adjectives could not sensibly be joined by *and*.

The house overflowed with *ornate electric* fixtures.
Among the junk in the attic was *one lovely* vase.

23f

(23f.) Commas with dates, addresses, place names, numbers

When they appear within sentences, elements punctuated with commas are also ended with commas.

Dates

On July 1, 1967, Canada celebrated its centennial.
[When a date begins with the month, place commas before *and* after the year.]
On 1 July 1967 Canada celebrated its centennial.
[When a date begins with the day, do not use any commas.]

Addresses and place names

Use the address 49 Front Street, St. John's, Newfoundland A1E 2Y2, for all correspondence. [No comma is needed between the name of the province and the postal code.]

Numbers (imperial system)
The new assembly plant cost $7,525,000.
A kilometre is 3,281 feet (*or* 3281 feet).

(23g.) Commas with quotations

A comma or commas usually separate a quotation from the words used to identify the source, such as *she said* or *he replied.*

> Marshall McLuhan said, "The medium is the message."

> "Knowledge is power," wrote Francis Bacon.

> "You don't need a weatherman," sings Bob Dylan, "to know which way the wind blows."

Do not use a comma when the identifying words interrupt the quotation between main clauses.° Instead, follow the identifying words with a semicolon or period.

> "That part of my life was over," she wrote; "his words had sealed it shut."

> "That part of my life was over," she wrote. "His words had sealed it shut."

24 The Semicolon

The semicolon separates equal and balanced sentence elements, usually complete sentences (main clauses°). Use it instead of a period to stress the connection between two main clauses.

(24a.) Semicolon between complete sentences not joined by *and, but, or, nor,* etc.

Between complete sentences

Use a semicolon between complete sentences (main clauses°) that are not connected by *and, but, or, nor, for, so,* or *yet* (the coordinating conjunctions°).

Increased taxes are only one way to pay for programs; cost cutting also frees up money.

Not between main clauses and subordinate elements

Do not use a semicolon between a main clause and a subordinate element, such as a subordinate clause° or a phrase.°

Not According to African authorities; only about 35,000 Pygmies exist today.

But According to African authorities, only about 35,000 Pygmies exist today.

Not Anthropologists have campaigned; for the protection of the Pygmies' habitat.

But Anthropologists have campaigned for the protection of the Pygmies' habitat.

(24b.) Semicolon with *however, thus, for example,* and so on

Use a semicolon between complete sentences (main clauses°) that are related by two kinds of words: conjunctive adverbs,° such as *hence, however, indeed, moreover, therefore,* and *thus;* and other transitional expressions,° such as *after all, for example, in fact,* and *of course.*

Blue jeans have become fashionable all over the world; *however,* the American originators still wear more jeans than anyone else.

A conjunctive adverb or transitional expression may move around within its clause, so the semicolon will not always come just before the adverb or expression. The adverb or expression itself is usually set off with a comma or commas.

Blue jeans have become fashionable all over the world; the American originators, *however,* still wear more jeans than anyone else.

(24c.) Semicolons with series

Between series items

Use semicolons (rather than commas) to separate items in a series when the items contain commas.

The custody case involved Amy Dalton, the child; Ellen and Mark Dalton, the parents; and Ruth and Hal Blum, the grandparents.

Not before a series

Do not use a semicolon to introduce a series. (Use a colon or a dash instead.)

Not   Teachers have heard all sorts of reasons why students do poorly; psychological problems, family illness, too much work, too little time.

But   Teachers have heard all sorts of reasons why students do poorly: psychological problems, family illness, too much work, too little time.

25 The Colon

The colon is mainly a mark of introduction, but it has a few other conventional uses as well.

25a. Colon for introduction

At end of main clause

The colon ends a complete sentence (main clause°) and introduces various additions:

The first warm days of spring, followed by cool nights, send an unmistakable message: it's time to visit the sugar bush. [Introduces an explanation.]

We look forward to a variety of maple products: syrup, toffee, fudge, maple butter, and maple sugar. [Introduces a series.]

The sugaring-off meal provides an essential ingredient for the men and women who work in the sugar bush: calories to fuel hard labour. [Introduces an appositive.°]

A farmer in the Beauce gives his helpers plenty of food: "We serve maple-glazed ham, eggs poached in maple syrup, and maple-baked beans. For dessert we offer sugar pie." [Introduces a long quotation.]

Not inside main clause

Do not use a colon inside a main clause, especially after *such as* or a verb.

Not The best-known maple product is: syrup. Outside Canada, few people have tasted some maple delicacies such as: toffee or *tire*.

But The best-known maple product is syrup. Outside Canada, few people have tasted some maple delicacies such as toffee or *tire*.

(25b.) Colon with salutations of business letters, titles and subtitles, divisions of time, and biblical citations

Salutation of a business letter
Dear Ms. Singh:

Title and subtitle
Anna Freud: *Her Life and Work*

Time
12:26   6:00

Biblical citation
1 Corinthians 3:6–7

26a

26 The Apostrophe

The apostrophe (') appears as part of a word to indicate possession, contraction (the omission of one or more letters), or (in a few cases) plural number.

(26a.) Apostrophe with possessives

The POSSESSIVE form of a word indicates that it owns or is the source of another word: *the dog's hair*, *everyone's hope*. For nouns° and indefinite pronouns,° such as *everyone,* the possessive form always includes an apostrophe and often an *-s*.

Note The apostrophe or apostrophe-plus-*s* is an *addition*. Before this addition, always spell the name of the owner or owners without dropping or adding letters.

Singular words: Add -'*s.*

Bill *Boughton's* skillful card tricks amaze children.

Anyone's eyes would widen.

The -'*s* ending for singular words pertains to singular words ending in -*s*.

Sandra *Cisneros's* work is highly regarded.

The *business's* customers filed suit.

Plural words ending in -*s:* Add -' only.

Workers' incomes have fallen slightly over the past year.

Many students take several *years'* leave after high school.

The *Murphys'* son lives at home.

Plural words not ending in -*s:* Add -'*s.*

Children's educations are at stake.

We need to attract the *media's* attention.

Compound words: Add -'*s* only to the last word.

The *brother-in-law's* business failed.

Taxes are always *somebody else's* fault.

Two or more owners: Add -'*s* depending on possession.

Youngman's and Mason's comedy techniques are similar. [Each comedian has his own technique.]

The child recovered despite her *mother and father's* neglect. [The mother and father were jointly neglectful.]

26b. Misuses of the apostrophe

Not with plural nouns°

Correct   The unleashed *dogs* belonged to the Joneses.

Not with singular verbs°

Correct   The subway *breaks* down less often now.

Not with possessives of personal pronouns°

Correct   The car is *hers*, not *theirs*. *Its* colour is red.

Note Don't confuse possessive pronouns and contractions: *its, your, their,* and *whose* are possessives. *It's,* *you're, they're,* and *who's* are contractions. If in doubt, try expanding the contraction: *who's = who is.* See below.

(26c.)   Apostrophe with contractions

A CONTRACTION replaces one or more letters, numbers, or words with an apostrophe.

it is	it's	cannot	can't
you are	you're	does not	doesn't
they are	they're	were not	weren't
who is	who's	class of 1997	class of '97

Note Don't misuse the four contractions on the left for the possessive pronouns° *its, your, their,* and *whose.*

(26d.)   Apostrophe with plural letters, numbers, and words named as words

You may cite a character or word as a word rather than use it for its meaning. When such an element is plural, add an apostrophe plus *-s.*

This sentence has too many <u>but</u>'s.

Remember to dot your <u>i</u>'s and cross your <u>t</u>'s.

At the end of each poem, the author had written two <u>3</u>'s.

Notice that the cited element is underlined or italicized, but the apostrophe and added *-s* are not.

27 Quotation Marks

Quotation marks—either double (" ") or single (' ')—mainly enclose direct quotations from speech and from writing.

This chapter treats the main uses of quotation marks. For when to use quotations from sources in a paper, see pp. 132–33. For how to integrate quotations into your own prose, see pp. 137–38. For punctuation to use when altering quotations, see pp. 93–95.

Note Quotation marks *always* come in pairs, one before and one after the quoted material.

27a. Quotation marks with direct quotations

Double quotation marks

A DIRECT QUOTATION° reports what someone said or wrote, in the exact words of the original.

"Life," said the psychoanalyst Karen Horney, "remains a very efficient therapist."

Note Do not use quotation marks with an indirect quotation, which reports what someone said or wrote but not in the exact words of the original.

Single quotation marks

Use single quotation marks to enclose a quotation within a quotation.

"In formulating any philosophy," Woody Allen writes, "the first consideration must always be: What can we know? . . . Descartes hinted at the problem when he wrote, 'My mind can never know my body, although it has become quite friendly with my leg.'"

Long quotations

Use an indention to set off long quotations from the main body of your text. *Do not use quotation marks with a set-off quotation.*

In his 1967 study of the lives of unemployed black men, Elliot Liebow observes that "unskilled" construction work requires more experience and skill than is generally assumed.

> A healthy, sturdy, active man of good intelligence requires from two to four weeks to break in on a construction job. . . . It frequently happens that his foreman or the craftsman he services is not willing to wait that long for him to get into condition or to learn at a glance the difference in size between a rough 2 x 8 and a finished 2 x 10. (62)

(The parenthetical number at the end of the quotation is a source citation.)

The length of a set-off quotation and method of displaying it vary among academic disciplines. Here are the formats recommended by the principal discipline guides:

English, other modern languages, and some other humanities (*MLA Style Manual and Guide to Scholarly Publishing,* second ed.): This is the style illustrated on page 88. Set off four or more lines of poetry and five or more typed lines of prose. Indent the quotation one inch or ten spaces from the left, double-space the quotation, and double-space above and below the quotation.

History, art history, and some other humanities (*The Chicago Manual of Style,* fourteenth ed., and the student guide adapted from it, Kate L. Turabian's *A Manual for Writers of Term Papers, Theses, and Dissertations,* sixth ed.): Set off poetry of more than two lines. Set off prose of more than four to ten lines, depending on your reason for quoting and the number of displayed quotations you have. (For instance, you might set off a number of shorter quotations when you are comparing them.) Indent any displayed quotation five spaces from the left, single-space the quotation, and double-space above and below it.

Psychology and some other disciplines (*Publication Manual of the American Psychological Association,* fifth ed.): Set off quotations of more than forty words. For student papers, indent the quotation five to seven spaces from the left, single-space the quotation, and double-space above and below the quotation.

27a

Life sciences, physical sciences, and mathematics (*Scientific Style and Format: The CBE Manual for Authors, Editors, and Publishers,* sixth ed. Revisions for the seventh edition of this book, to be published by the Council for Science Editors—formerly the Council for Biology Editors—were under way when this book went to press. For more information, visit the CSE website at *www.councilscienceeditors.org/.*) This guide specifies only that long quotations be set off and indented, so any of the formats above is appropriate.

Dialogue

When quoting a conversation, put the speeches in double quotation marks and begin a new paragraph for each speaker.

> "What shall I call you? Your name?" Andrews whispered rapidly, as with a high squeak the latch of the door rose.
> "Elizabeth," she said. "Elizabeth."
> —GRAHAM GREENE, *The Man Within*

27b. Quotation marks with titles of works

Within your text use quotation marks to enclose the titles of works that are published or released within larger works (see below). Use <u>underlining</u> or *italics* for all other titles (see p. 116).

Song
"Satisfaction"

Short story
"The Loons"

Short poem
"The Double Voice"

Article in a periodical
"Does 'Scaring' Work?"

Essay
"Joey: A 'Mechanical Boy'"

Episode of a television or radio program
"Dieppe" (on <u>Canada at War</u>)

Subdivision of a book
"The Mast Head" (Chapter 35 of <u>Moby Dick</u>)

Note Some academic disciplines do not require quotation marks for titles within source citations. See pages 166–78 (APA style) and 178–82 (CBE style).

27c. Quotation marks for words used in a special sense

On movie sets, movable "wild walls" make a one-walled room seem four-walled on film.

27d. Quotation marks with other punctuation

Commas and periods: inside quotation marks

Jonathan Swift wrote a famous satire, "A Modest Proposal," in 1729.

"Swift's 'A Modest Proposal,'" wrote one critic, "is so outrageous that it cannot be believed."

Colons and semicolons: outside quotation marks

A few years ago the slogan in elementary education was "learning by playing"; now educators focus on basic skills.

We all know the meaning of "basic skills": reading, writing, and arithmetic.

Dashes, question marks, and exclamation points: inside quotation marks only if part of the quotation

When a dash, question mark, or exclamation point is part of the quotation, place it *inside* quotation marks. Don't use any other punctuation, such as a period or comma.

"But must you—" Marcia hesitated, afraid of the answer.

The stranger asked, "Where am I?"

"Go away!" I yelled.

When a dash, question mark, or exclamation point applies only to the larger sentence, not to the quotation, place it *outside* quotation marks—again, with no other punctuation.

Betty Friedan's question in 1963—"Who knows what women can be?"—encouraged generations of women to seek answers.

Who said, "Now cracks a noble heart"?

The woman called me "stupid"!

When both the quotation and the larger sentence take a question mark or exclamation point, use only the one *inside* the quotation mark.

Did you say, "Who is she?"

28 Other Marks

The other marks of punctuation are the dash, parentheses, the ellipsis mark, brackets, and the slash.

(28a.) Dash or dashes for shifts and interruptions

The dash (—) punctuates sentences. In contrast, the hyphen (-) punctuates words. Form a dash with two hyphens (—). Do not add extra space before, after, or between the hyphens.

Shifts in tone or thought

The novel—if one could call it that—appeared in 1994.

If the book had a plot—but a plot would be too conventional.

Non-essential elements

You may use dashes instead of commas to set off and emphasize elements that are not essential to the meaning of your sentence (see p. 79). Be sure to use a pair of dashes when the element interrupts the sentence.

The qualities Monet painted—sunlight, rich shadows, deep colours—abounded near the rivers and gardens he used as subjects.

Introductory series and concluding series and explanations

Shortness of breath, skin discolouration, persistent indigestion, the presence of small lumps—all these may signify cancer. [Introductory series.]

The patient undergoes a battery of tests—CT scan, bronchoscopy, perhaps even biopsy. [Concluding series.]

Many patients are disturbed by the CT scan—by the need to keep still for long periods in an exceedingly small space. [Concluding explanation.]

You may use a colon (p. 184) instead of a dash in the last two examples. The dash is more informal.

(28b.) Parentheses for non-essential elements

Parentheses always come in pairs, one before and one after the punctuated material.

Parenthetical expressions

Parentheses de-emphasize PARENTHETICAL EXPRESSIONS—explanatory, supplemental, or transitional words or phrases. (Commas emphasize these expressions more and dashes still more.)

> Frederick Banting (later Sir Frederick Banting) and Charles Best discovered insulin in 1923.

Don't put a comma before a parenthetical expression enclosed in parentheses. Punctuation after the parenthetical expression should be placed outside the closing parenthesis.

Not   Although he did not receive the Nobel Prize, Charles Best had worked very closely with Frederick Banting, (later Sir Frederick Banting.)

But   Although he did not receive the Nobel Prize, Charles Best had worked very closely with Frederick Banting (later Sir Frederick Banting).

Labels for lists

> The Nobel Prize for the discovery of insulin was awarded to (1) Frederick Banting, (2) J. J. R. Macleod, and (3) James B. Collip.

28c

(28c.) ## Ellipsis mark for omissions from quotations

The ellipsis mark consists of three spaced periods (. . .). It generally indicates an omission from a quotation, as illustrated in the following excerpts from this quotation about the Philippines:

Original quotation

"It was the Cuba of the future. It was going the way of Iran. It was another Nicaragua, another Cambodia, another Vietnam. But all these places, awesome in their histories, are so different from each other that one couldn't help thinking: this kind of talk was a shorthand for a confusion. All that was being said was that something was happening in the Philippines. Or more plausibly, a lot of different things were happening in the Philippines. And a lot of people were feeling obliged to speak out about it."

—JAMES FENTON, "The Philippine Election"

Omission of the middle of a sentence

"But all these places . . . are so different from each other that one couldn't help thinking: this kind of talk was a shorthand for a confusion."

Omission of the end of a sentence

"It was another Nicaragua. . . ." [The sentence period, close up to the last word, precedes the ellipsis mark.]

"It was another Nicaragua . . ." (Fenton 25). [When the quotation is followed by a parenthetical source citation, as here, the sentence period follows the citation.]

Omission of parts of two sentences

"All that was being said was that . . . a lot of different things were happening in the Philippines."

Omission of one or more sentences

"It was the Cuba of the future. It was going the way of Iran. It was another Nicaragua, another Cambodia, another Vietnam. . . . All that was being said was that something was happening in the Philippines."

Brackets with ellipsis

Some instructors require students to follow the previous MLA style of inserting all ellipses in square brackets. Leave one space before the opening bracket and leave one space after the closing bracket unless the ellipsis is immediately followed by a punctuation mark. Do not leave any spaces between the brackets and the ellipsis:

"It was another Nicaragua [. . .]" (Fenton 25).

"Leanora [. . .] asked for the goblet."

Always insert *your* ellipsis within brackets to distinguish it from an ellipsis in the original source, even if your instructor does not normally require brackets:

"I wonder why. . . . [. . .] Now I will never know."

Note these features of the examples:

- The ellipsis mark indicates that material is omitted from the source when the omission would not otherwise be clear. Don't use an ellipsis mark when it's clear you are not quoting a full sentence: *Fenton calls the Philippines "another Nicaragua."*
- After a grammatically complete sentence, an ellipsis mark usually follows a sentence period and a space (second and fifth examples). The exception occurs when a parenthetical source citation follows the quotation (third example), in which case the sentence period falls after the citation.

If you omit one or more lines of poetry or paragraphs of prose from a quotation, use a separate line of ellipsis marks across the full width of the quotation to show the omission.

Brackets for changes in quotations

Brackets have highly specialized uses in mathematical equations, but their main use for all kinds of writing is to indicate that you have altered a quotation to explain, clarify, or correct it.

"This Petrocan station [just outside Calgary] is the cleanest in Canada," boasted the manager.

Slash for options and between lines of poetry

Option

Some teachers oppose pass/fail courses.

Between lines of poetry

When you run two lines of poetry into your text, separate them with a slash surrounded by space.

Many readers have sensed a reluctant turn away from death in Frost's lines "The woods are lovely, dark and deep, / But I have promises to keep."

28e

V Conventions of Form and Appearance

Checklist for Form and Appearance

✓ Document Design

Have you used the elements of design—such as type, margins, headings, and illustrations—to produce a clear and attractive document? (See pp. 99–112.)

✓ Spelling

Are all your words spelled correctly? Don't rely on your spell-checker to answer this question. (See pp. 121–22.)

✓ Capital letters

Have you used capital letters appropriately for proper nouns and adjectives and for the titles of works and persons? (See pp. 114–16.)

✓ Underlining or italics

Have you used underlining or italics primarily for the titles of works published separately from other works? Does your use of underlining or italics in source citations conform to your discipline's or instructor's requirements? (See pp. 116–17.)

✓ Abbreviations

Have you used abbreviations appropriately for the discipline or field you are writing in? (See pp. 118–20.)

✓ Numbers

Have you expressed numbers in numerals or words appropriately for the discipline or field you are writing in? (See pp. 120–21.)

29 Document Format

Legible, consistent, and attractive papers and correspondence serve your readers and reflect well on you. This chapter shows the basics of formatting any document clearly and effectively (29a), provides design guidelines for academic papers in various disciplines (29b), and discusses formats for business correspondence such as job-application letters, résumés, and electronic mail (29c).

(29a.) Clear and effective documents

Your papers, reports, and correspondence must of course be neat and legible. That means, at a minimum, a readable typeface, adequate margins, and very few, if any, corrections. But you can do more to make your work accessible and attractive, especially if you work on a computerized word processor. You can use paper, type, white space, headings, lists, and illustrations to put your ideas across efficiently and forcefully.

Paper

Unless your project demands otherwise, use 8½" × 11" white bond paper of at least 16-lb. weight, and use the same type of paper throughout a project. Type or print on only one side of each sheet.

Type

Print quality

Type or print all documents. (Handwriting may be acceptable in some academic assignments, but always check with your instructor before submitting a handwritten paper.) Use black type, making sure that the printer's ribbon or cartridge is fresh enough to produce a dark impression.

Text

Academic papers are generally double-spaced; business writing is often single-spaced. See pages 104–108 and 108–112, respectively, for more on the spacing of lines.

The type for the text of your document should be at least 10 or 12 points, as illustrated by these type samples:

`12-point Courier` 12-point Times Roman
`10-point Courier`   10-point Times Roman

Avoid unusual or decorative fonts. Use one space between words and after most punctuation, including the punctuation at the ends of sentences. (For the special spacing with ellipsis marks, which show omissions from quotations, see pp. 93–94.) Type a dash with two hyphens (--). Use handwriting to make symbols that are not on your keyboard.

Within the text use <u>underlining</u>, *italics,* or **boldface** to emphasize key words or sentences (see Chapter 32). For academic research writing, ask your instructor whether he or she prefers underlining or italics with source citations. Note that many readers consider the constant use of type embellishments to be distracting. Vary type selectively to enhance your meaning, not just to decorate your work.

Long quotations

Set off long quotations according to the guidelines for various disciplines on pages 88–89.

Source citations

If you need to cite sources for your work, follow one of the systems discussed in Chapter 43, as appropriate for the field you're writing in.

29a

Corrections

Business correspondence should be error-free, without visible corrections. Academic writing permits some corrections. Make your corrections *neatly,* either by typing or by hand in black ink. If a page has more than a few errors, reprint it.

White space, headings, and lists

The white space on a page eases crowding, highlights elements, and focuses readers' attention.

Paragraph breaks

An indention at the beginning of a paragraph (in double-spaced copy) or extra space between paragraphs (in single-spaced copy) gives readers a break and reassures them that you have divided ideas into manageable chunks.

Margins

Use minimum one-inch margins on all sides of every page. Use a larger left margin if you plan to bind the document on the left. An uneven right margin is almost always acceptable. If your word processor will produce an even (or justified) right margin, use the feature only if it does not sometimes leave wide spaces between words, and then only for formal, public documents, not correspondence or academic assignments.

Headings

In a research paper, business report, or similarly long and complex document, headings within the text can clarify organization and the relationships among parts. When you use headings, follow these guidelines:

- Create an outline of your document in order to plan where headings should go. Inconsistent, overlapping, or missing headings do more harm than good.
- Keep headings as short as possible while making them specific about the material that follows.
- Word headings consistently—for instance, all questions (*What Is the Scientific Method?*), all phrases° with *-ing* words (*Understanding the Scientific Method*), or all phrases with nouns (*The Scientific Method*).
- Indicate the relative importance of headings with type size, positioning, and highlighting, such as capital letters and underlining.

<pre>
             FIRST-LEVEL HEADING

Second-Level Heading

Third-Level Heading
</pre>

FIRST-LEVEL HEADING

Second-Level Heading

Third-Level Heading

- Keep the appearance simple: most reports or papers shouldn't need more than two type styles or two or three type sizes (including the body type). Avoid extra-large letters and unusual styles of type (such as outline and shadow type).
- Don't break a page immediately after a heading. Push the heading to the next page.

Note Document format in psychology and some other social sciences requires a particular treatment of headings. See page 106.

Lists

Whenever your document contains a list of related items—for example, the steps in a process or the elements in a proposal—consider setting the items off and marking them with numbers or bullets (centred dots,

29a

used in the list below about tables and illustrations). A list is easier to read than a paragraph and adds white space to the page. Most word-processing programs can format a numbered or bulleted list automatically.

Tables and illustrations

Tables and illustrations (graphs, charts, diagrams, photographs) can often make a point for you more efficiently and effectively than words can. Tables and illustrations present data, make comparisons, explain processes, show changes, and represent what something looks like, among other uses. Whatever kind of table or illustration you plan, follow these guidelines:

- Focus on a purpose for the table or illustration—a single point you want it to make. Otherwise, it may be too complex and may confuse readers.
- Provide a title for the table or illustration so that the reader knows immediately what its purpose and content are. Generally, a table's title falls above the table, whereas an illustration's title falls below.
- Make the table or illustration legible and attractive.
- Provide clear labels for all parts, such as columns and rows in a table, bars in a graph, and parts of a machine in a drawing. In the interest of clarity, avoid abbreviations unless you know your readers will understand them.
- Provide a source note whenever the data or the entire table or illustration is someone else's independent material (see pp. 133–36). Each discipline has a slightly different style for such source notes; those in the table on page 103 and the figures on pages 103–104 reflect the style of the social sciences. See also chapters 44–47.
- Number tables and figures separately (Table 1, Table 2, etc.; Figure 1, Figure 2, etc.).
- Refer to each table or figure (for instance, "See Figure 2") at the point(s) in the text where readers will benefit by consulting it.
- Unless your document includes many tables and/or illustrations, place each one on a page by itself immediately after the page that refers to it.

Many organizations and academic disciplines have preferred styles for tables and figures that may differ from those presented here. When in doubt about how to prepare and place tables and illustrations, ask your instructor or supervisor.

29a

Tables

Tables usually summarize raw data, displaying the data concisely and clearly.

Table 1
Incidence of Courtship Violence

Type of violence	Number of students reporting	Percentage of sample
Insulted or swore	62	50.4
Threatened to hit or throw something	17	13.8
Threw something	8	6.5
Pushed, grabbed, or shoved	18	14.6
Slapped	8	6.6
Kicked, bit, or hit with fist	7	5.7
Hit or tried to hit with something	2	1.6
Threatened with a knife or gun	1	0.8
Used a knife or gun	1	0.8

Note. Data from "Recent Increases in Dating Violence," by M. Laner, 1983, Social Problems, 22, p. 160.

Illustrations

Illustrations often recast data into visual form. Pie charts, bar graphs, and line graphs are helpful for comparisons, such as changes and proportions.

29a

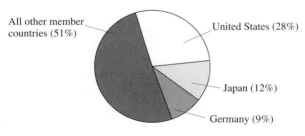

Figure 1. Member countries' assessments to United Nations budget of $1.1 billion in 1994. From "The U.N. at 50," by R. Mylan, 1995, October 18, *Newsweek,* p. 17.

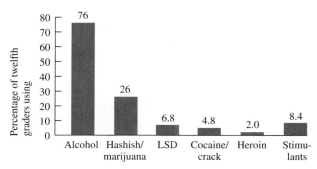

Figure 2. Use of alcohol, compared to other drugs, among twelfth graders (1993). Data from *Monitoring the Future study*, 1994, Ann Arbor, MI: University of Michigan Press.

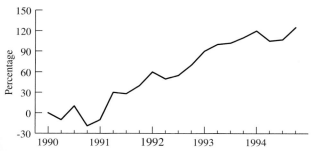

Figure 3. Five-year cumulative return for equities in Standard & Poor's 500 Index, 1990–1994.

Note Graphics software and some word-processing software will create tables, graphs, charts, and other illustrations when you supply the raw data. If you use many tables and illustrations in your writing, you'll find it worthwhile to master computerized graphics.

29b. Academic papers

The principles of document format discussed in section 29a apply generally to academic writing, but most disciplines require specific variations to suit the needs of their research and writing.

English, other modern languages, and some other humanities: MLA format

The style guide for English and some other humanities is the *MLA Handbook for Writers of Research*

Papers, 6th edition (2003), and the *MLA Style Manual and Guide to Scholarly Publishing*, 2nd edition (1998), both published by the Modern Language Association. These guides recommend a document format like the one discussed in section 29a for paper, type, margins, and illustrations.

Number all pages, starting with 1 for the first page and continuing in sequence through any endnotes and the list of works cited. Add your last name just before each page number, as illustrated by "Jacobs" in the samples.

First page of paper

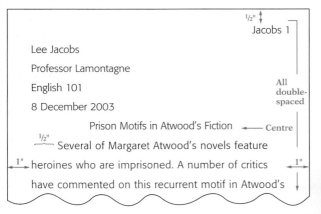

Later page of paper

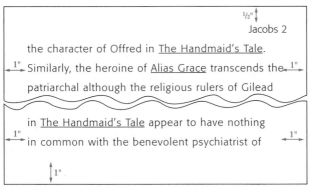

Note For MLA style for long quotations set off from the text, see section 25a. For MLA style for source citations, see Chapter 44.

History, art history, philosophy, and some other humanities: *Chicago Manual* format

The Chicago Manual of Style, fifteenth edition (2003), serves as a style guide for history, art history, philosophy, and some other humanities. A guide for students adapted from *The Chicago Manual* is Kate L. Turabian, *A Manual for Writers of Term Papers, Theses, and Dissertations,* sixth edition, revised by John Grossman and Alice Bennett (1996). The document format discussed in section 29a resembles those recommended by both of these books. For spacing and arranging elements, use the MLA format illustrated on p. 105, with the following exceptions:

- Number pages with a number only, consecutively from the first page through the entire paper. On the first page of the paper and the first page of any end-notes and the bibliography, place the page number at the bottom of the page, centred. On all other pages, place the number at the top, either centred or at the right margin, and double-space to the text below.
- Capitalize the title, and triple-space beneath it.
- *A Manual for Writers* suggests a separate title page, table of contents, and other preliminary elements for long, multi-chapter works. Consult the guide if your project or your instructor requires such elements.

Note See page 89 for *Chicago Manual* and *Manual for Writers* style for long quotations set off from the text. And see pages 159–66 for this style for source citations.

29b

Psychology and some other social sciences: APA format

The style guide for psychology, educational psychology, and some other social sciences is the *Publication Manual of the American Psychological Association,* fifth edition (2001). APA document format for student papers corresponds closely to the guidelines in section 29a, with some exceptions shown on the following samples.

Number the pages consecutively, beginning with 1 for the title page and continuing through the reference list. Five spaces before each page number, provide a shortened version of your title ("Dating Violence" in the samples).

For headings in social science papers, use these formats, always double-spacing:

First-Level Heading

<u>Second-Level Heading</u>

   <u>Third-level heading.</u> Run this heading into the text paragraph.

Title page

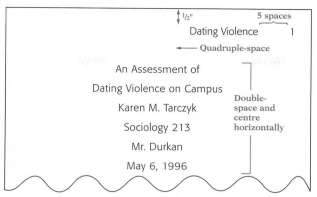

Abstract (summary in 120 words of subject, methods, findings, conclusions)

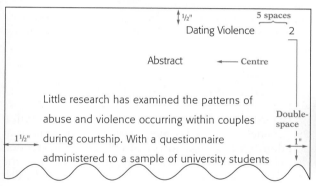

29b

First page of body

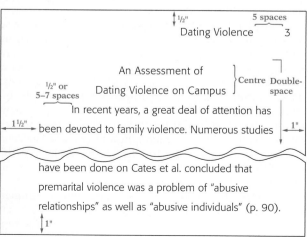

Note See page 89 for the APA style for long quotations set off from the text. And see pages 166–78 for APA style for source citations.

Life sciences, physical sciences, and mathematics: CBE style

The style guide for the life sciences and often for the physical sciences and mathematics is *Scientific Style and Format: The CBE Manual for Authors, Editors, and Publishers,* 6th edition (1994), published for The Council of Science Editors—formerly The Council of Biology Editors. The 7th edition was being prepared as this book went to press. For further information, consult *www.councilscienceeditors.org.* For student papers (as opposed to those planned for publication), use a format like that shown for APA style (pp. 106–108), including title page and abstract. (You may omit the shortened title before the page number.)

Note For CBE style for long quotations set off from the text, see page 89. For CBE style for source citations, see pages 178–82.

(29c.) Business correspondence

The essential document format discussed in section 29a applies to most business writing, with important additions for headings and other elements. This section discusses the business letter, using the example of the job-application letter, and the résumé. It also briefly discusses electronic mail, which has a format of its own.

Job-application letter

In any letter to a businessperson, you are addressing someone who wants to see quickly why you are writing and how to respond to you. For a job application, announce right off what job you are applying for and how you heard about it. (See the sample letter on the next page.) Summarize your qualifications for the job, including facts about your education and employment history that qualify you for the job. Don't recite what's on the résumé; instead, highlight and reshape the relevant parts of the résumé for the particular job. At the end of the letter, mention when you are available for an interview and provide your phone number.

For business correspondence, use either unlined white paper measuring 8½" × 11" (21.5 cm × 28 cm), letterhead stationery with your address printed at the top,

367 rue des Erables
Verdun, Quebec H3E 1W6
17 February 2003

Director of Human Resources
SNC-Lavalin Inc.
1100 Blvd. René-Lévesque West
Montreal, Quebec H3B 4P3

Dear Director of Human Resources:

In response to your advertisement in the <u>Montreal Gazette</u>, I am applying for the position of surveyor.

I am completing my final year of civil engineering studies at Dawson College and will receive my Diploma of Collegial Studies in June 2003.

While at Dawson College I remained on the honour roll for six semesters, earning a grade average of 86.4 percent. As president of the Civil Tech Club from 2001 to 2003, I was instrumental in organizing an engineering fair for civil tech students. My work experience at the Royal Victoria Hospital demonstrates that I possess the discipline and personal skills that your company seeks. I am also fully bilingual.

As my enclosed résumé shows, I have the education and experience you are looking for.

I am available for an interview at your convenience. Please call me at 288-4783.

Yours sincerely,

Anna DiMaio

Anna DiMaio

Enc: Résumé

29c

or customized letterhead formatted on your computer. Type the letter single-spaced (with double spacing between elements and paragraphs), with no paragraph indents. Use one side of the sheet only, following the model on the previous page unless you choose the growing practice of aligning all elements with the left margin.

For the salutation, which greets the addressee, use a job title (*Dear Personnel Manager*) or use a general salutation (*Dear Sir or Madam*)—unless of course you know the addressee's name. When addressing a woman by name, use *Ms.* when she has no other title, when you don't know how she prefers to be addressed, or when you know she prefers *Ms.* For the letter's close, choose an expression that reflects the formality in the salutation: *Respectfully, Cordially, Yours truly,* and *Sincerely* are more formal than *Regards* and *Best wishes.*

The envelope should show your name and address in the upper-left corner and the addressee's name, title, and address in the centre. Use an envelope that will accommodate the letter once it is folded horizontally in thirds.

Résumé

The résumé that you enclose with a letter of application should contain, in table form, your name and address, career objective, and education and employment histories, along with information about how to obtain your references. Since every profession and every job has slightly different requirements, create a new résumé for each application. (A sample appears on the next page.) Use headings to mark the various sections of the résumé, spacing around them and within sections so that important information stands out. Try to limit your résumé to one page so that it can be quickly scanned. However, if your experience and education are extensive, a two-page résumé is preferable to a single cramped, unreadable page. Some companies receive and scan résumés electronically. To make your résumé scannable, use standard fonts, limit yourself to one or two font sizes, avoid formatting with bullets, and use easily recognizable keywords for each point. Since, however, you hope that an employer will read your résumé, write for a person, not a computer scanner.

In preparing your résumé, you may wish to consult one of the many books devoted to application letters, résumés, and other elements of a job search. Two helpful guides are Richard N. Bolles, *What Color Is Your Parachute? A Practical Manual for Job-Hunters and Career Changers,* and Tom Jackson, *The Perfect Résumé.*

29c

Anna DiMaio
367 rue des Erables
Verdun, Quebec H3E 1W6
Telephone: 514-288-4783
email: adimaio@dawsoncollege.qc.ca
Languages: English, French, Italian, some Spanish

Position desired
Surveyor, with possibility of career development, including university studies in civil engineering.

Education

2000–03	**Civil Engineering Technology, Dawson College**, D.E.C. to be completed June 2003 President, Civil Tech Club 2001–03 Honour Roll
1995–2000	**Centennial Regional High School**, Greenfield Park, Quebec DES completed June 2000

Technical Knowledge

Surveying:	Theodolites, Levels, Transits, Total Stations
Drafting:	manual, computer (ACAD 2002)
Estimating:	quantity take-offs
Software:	WordPerfect 2002, Windows 2000, Timberline (Estimating), Primavera (Project Management), Softdesk Energ. 7.2, Microsoft Word 2000
Laboratory testing:	concrete, soils, asphalt, aggregates

Employment History

2002–03	**Assistant Laboratory Technician, Dawson College** Organized and directed laboratory affairs, monitored laboratory tests, cleaned and reorganized after laboratory tests
2001–03	**Admitting and Discharge Clerk, Royal Victoria Hospital** Admitted patients, booked surgery time for patients, booked beds for patients

29c

References

Academic:	Mr. Howard Babcock, Chair Civil Engineering Technology Dept. Dawson College 3040 Sherbrooke Street West Westmount, Quebec H3Z 1A4
Employment:	Ms. Lise Dufresne Royal Victoria Hospital 687 Pine Avenue West Montreal, Quebec H3A 1A1
Personal:	Dr. Carole Adilman 9871 Gouin Blvd. West Pierrefonds, Quebec H8Y 1R9

Electronic mail

Electronic mail is usually more informal and often more terse than other business correspondence. Provide a clear subject line to tell your reader what your message contains. Within the message, use conventional paragraphing and white space between paragraphs to increase readability. In a long message, consider using headings to break up the text and direct your readers' attention.

Some email programs do not allow underlining, italics, or boldface, so you can't emphasize or highlight words conventionally. Alternatives include asterisks before and after the words to be highlighted (*I *will not* be able to attend the meeting*) or an underscore before and after a book title (*The book is _Public Relations_*). Avoid using all-capital letters for emphasis: they yell too loudly. An email message entirely in capital letters may be considered rude, no matter what its content. When using the "Reply" or "Forward" functions, delete inappropriate portions of the original message and update the subject line.

Note Business writing increasingly favours simplified style and format. To simplify letters, memos, and email messages, eliminate the salutation and complimentary close, especially if the recipient's identity is unknown, and use short sentences and contractions for readability. Type all elements flush with the left margin. To gain attention, insert a subject line in capital letters three lines below the inside address and three lines above the first paragraph:

Weak   Notice of Meeting

Effective MEETING TUESDAY TO APPROVE PRO-MOTION BUDGET

30 The Hyphen

Always use a hyphen to divide a word between syllables from one line to the next. Also use it to form some compound words, such as *cross-reference*, that express a combination of ideas. The following rules cover many but not all compounds. When you doubt the spelling of a compound word, consult a dictionary.

(30a.) Compound adjectives

When two or more words serve together as a single modifier° before a noun, a hyphen forms the modifying words clearly into a unit.

She is a *well-known* actor.

No *English-speaking* people were in the room.

When such a compound modifier follows the noun, the hyphen is unnecessary.

The actor is *well known*.

Those people are *English speaking*.

The hyphen is also unnecessary in a compound modifier containing an *-ly* adverb, even before the noun: *clearly defined terms*.

(30b.) Fractions and compound numbers

Hyphens join the parts of fractions: *three-fourths, one-half*. And the whole numbers *twenty-one* to *ninety-nine* are always hyphenated.

30c

(30c.) Prefixes and suffixes

Prefixes are usually attached to word stems without hyphens: *predetermine, unnatural, disengage*. However, a hyphen usually separates the two when the prefix precedes a capitalized word, when a capital letter is combined with a word, or when the combination links two of the same vowel or three of the same consonant in a way that could cause misreading: *un-American, A-frame, de-emphasize, trill-like*. And some prefixes, such as *self-, all-,* and *ex-* (meaning "formerly"), usually require hyphens no matter what follows: *self-control, all-inclusive, ex-student*. The only suffix that regularly requires a hyphen is *–elect*, as in *president-elect*.

31 Capital Letters

The following conventions and a desk dictionary can help you decide whether to capitalize a particular word. In general, capitalize only when a rule or the dictionary says you must.

Note The social, natural, and applied sciences require specialized capitalization for terminology, such as *Conditions A and B* or *Escherichia coli*. Consult one of the style guides listed on pages 142–43 for the requirements of the discipline you are writing in.

31a. First word of a sentence

Every writer should own a good dictionary.

31b. Proper nouns and adjectives

Proper nouns name specific persons, places, and things: *Shakespeare, Alberta, World War I*. Proper adjectives are formed from some proper nouns: *Shakespearean, Albertan*. Capitalize all proper nouns and proper adjectives but not the articles (*a, an, the*) that precede them.

Specific persons and things
Pierre Berton   Rideau Canal

Specific places and geographical regions
Halifax   the North, the Maritimes
But: north of the city, a maritime climate

Days of the week, months, holidays
Monday   Yom Kippur
May   Christmas

Historical events, documents, periods, movements
the Meech Lake Accord   the Renaissance
the 1837 Rebellion   the Fenians

Government offices or departments and institutions
House of Commons   Supreme Court
Canada Council   Centennial Collegiate High
                                 School

31b

Political, social, athletic, and other organizations and their members

B'nai B'rith	Liberal Party, Liberals
Rotary Club	Toronto Blue Jays
National Farmers Union	Montreal Symphony Orchestra

Races, nationalities, and their languages

First Nations, Aboriginal peoples	Germans
African-Canadian	Swahili
Caucasian	Ukrainian
But: blacks, whites	

Religions, their followers, and terms for the sacred

Christianity, Christians	God
Catholicism, Catholics	Allah
Judaism, Orthodox Jew	the Bible (*but* biblical)
Islam, Muslims *or* Moslems	the Qur'an or Koran

Common nouns as parts of proper nouns

Main Street	Lake Superior
Spadina Avenue	Ford Motor Company
Stanley Park	Memorial University
Great Slave Lake	Prince Edward County
Pacific Ocean	Jacques Cartier Bridge

But: the lake, university course, the company, the bridge

31c. Titles and subtitles of works

Within your text, capitalize all the words in a title and subtitle *except* the following: articles (*a, an, the*), *to* in infinitives,° and connecting words (prepositions° and conjunctions°) of fewer than five letters. Capitalize even these short words when they are the first or last word in a title or when they fall after a colon or semicolon.

Voyage of the Iceberg	*Swann: A Literary Mystery*
"The Albanian Virgin"	*To the Lighthouse*
File Under Architecture	"Knowing Whom to Ask"

Note Some academic disciplines require a different treatment of titles within source citations, such as capitalizing only the first words of some or all titles. See pages 166–78 (APA style) and 178–82 (CBE style).

31d. Titles of persons

Before a person's name, capitalize his or her title. After the name, do not capitalize the title.

Professor Otto Osborne   Otto Osborne, a professor
Doctor Jane Covington   Jane Covington, a doctor
Judge Alan B. Gold   Alan B. Gold, the judge

32 Underlining (Italics)

Underlining and *italic type* indicate the same thing: the word or words are being distinguished or emphasized. In business the almost universal use of computerized word processors makes both forms of highlighting possible, and italics may be preferred. In schools the use of italics is becoming common, but some disciplines continue to require underlining for works in source citations. Consult your instructor before you use italic type.

Note   If you underline two or more words in a row, underline the space between the words, too: Criminal Statistics: Misuses of Numbers.

32a. Titles of works

Within your text, underline or italicize the titles of works, such as books and periodicals, that are published, released, or produced separately from other works. (See below.) Use quotation marks for all other titles, such as short stories and articles in periodicals. (See p. 90.)

Book
War and Peace

Long poem
Paradise Lost

Play
Hamlet

Periodical
The Hamilton Spectator

Pamphlet
The Truth About
    Alcoholism

Published speech
Lincoln's Gettysburg
    Address

Long musical work
The Beatles' Revolver
But: Symphony in C

Television or radio program
Choral Concert

Work of visual art
Michelangelo's David

Movie
Margaret's Museum

Exceptions Legal documents, the Bible, and their parts are generally not underlined.

Correct We studied the Book of Revelation in the New English Bible.

Note Some academic disciplines do not require underlining or italics for some or all titles within source citations. See pages 166–78 (APA style) and 178–82 (CBE style).

32b. Ships, aircraft, spacecraft, trains

| Challenger | Orient Express | Queen Elizabeth 2 |
| Apollo XI | Montrealer | Cariboo |

32c. Non-English words

Underline a non-English expression that has not been absorbed into our language. A dictionary will say whether a word is still considered foreign to English.

The scientific name for the brown trout is <u>Salmo trutta</u>. [The Latin scientific names for plants and animals are always underlined.]

In Quebec, a convenience store is called a <u>dépanneur</u> by English and French alike.

32d

32d. Words, letters, and numbers named as words

Underline characters or words that are cited as words rather than used for their meanings.

Some people pronounce <u>th</u>, as in <u>thought</u>, with a faint <u>s</u> or <u>f</u> sound.

The word <u>syzygy</u> refers to a straight line formed by three celestial bodies, as in the alignment of the earth, sun, and moon. [Quotation marks may also be used for words being defined.]

33 Abbreviations

The following guidelines on abbreviations pertain to the text of a non-technical document. All academic disciplines use abbreviations in source citations, and much technical writing, such as in the sciences and engineering, uses many abbreviations in the document text. See chapters 41–44 on source citations. Consult one of the style guides listed on pages 142–43 for the in-text requirements of the discipline you are writing in.

Note Usage varies, but writers increasingly omit periods from abbreviations of two or more words written in all-capital letters: *NWT, BA, UBC.* See page 77.

33a. Titles before and after proper names

Before the name	After the name
Dr. James Hsu	James Hsu, MD
Mr., Mrs., Ms., Hon.,	DDS, DVM, Ph.D.,
St., Rev., Msgr., Gen.	Ed.D., OSB, SJ, Sr., Jr.

Do not use abbreviations such as *Rev., Hon., Prof., Rep., Sen., Dr.,* and *St.* (for *Saint*) unless they appear before a proper name.

33b. Familiar abbreviations

Abbreviations using initials are acceptable in most writing as long as they are familiar to readers.

Institutions	UN, AGO, UNB
Organizations	CUPE, YMCA, NDP, IATA
Corporations	IBM, CN, CTV
People	JFK, FDR
Countries	U.S.A. (or USA)

Note If a name or term (such as *operating room*) appears often in a piece of writing, then its abbreviation (*OR*) can cut down on extra words. Spell out the full term at its first appearance, indicate its abbreviation in parentheses, and then use the abbreviation.

(33c.) *BC, AD, AM, PM, no.,* and *$*

Use certain abbreviations only with specific dates or numbers.

44 BC	11:26 AM (*or* a.m.)	no. 36 (*or* No. 36)
AD 1492	8:05 PM (*or* p.m.)	$7.41

The abbreviation BC ("before Christ") always follows a date, whereas AD (*anno Domini,* Latin for "in the year of the Lord") precedes a date.

Note BCE ("before the common era") and CE ("common era") are increasingly replacing BC and AD, respectively. Both follow the date.

(33d.) Latin abbreviations

Generally, use the common Latin abbreviations (without underlining) only in source citations and comments in parentheses.

i.e.	*id est:* that is
cf.	*confer:* compare
e.g.	*exempli gratia:* for example
et al.	*et alii:* and others
etc.	*et cetera:* and so forth
NB	*nota bene:* note well

He said he would be gone a fortnight (i.e., two weeks).
Bloom et al., editors, *Anthology of Light Verse*

(33e.) Words usually spelled out

In most academic, general, and business writing, certain words should always be spelled out. (In technical writing, however, these words are more often abbreviated.)

Note Always spell out *and* (rather than using *&*) unless the symbol appears in a business name.

Units of measurement
The dog is thirty *inches* [not *in.*] high.
It once swam two *kilometres* [not *km*] across a lake.

Geographical names
The publisher is in *Massachusetts* [not *Mass.* or *MA*].
It moved from *Canada* [not *Can.*].

33e

Names of days, months, and holidays

The truce was signed on *Tuesday* [not *Tues.*], *April* [not *Apr.*] 16.

It was ratified by *Christmas* [not *Xmas*].

Names of people

Robert [not *Robt.*] Frost writes accessible poems.

Virginia [not *Va.*] Woolf was British.

Courses of instruction

The writer teaches *political science* [not *poli. sci.*].

She received an *economics* [not *econ.*] degree.

34 Numbers

This chapter addresses the use of numbers (numerals versus words) in the text of a document. All disciplines use many more numerals in source citations (see chapters 41–44).

34a. Numerals vs. words

Always use numerals for numbers that require more than two words to spell out.

The leap year has *366* days.

The population of Yellowknife is about *18,100.*

In non-technical academic writing, spell out numbers of one or two words.

The hockey game drew *twenty-three thousand* people. [A hyphenated number may be considered one word.]

In much business writing, use numerals for all numbers over ten (*five reasons, 11 participants*). In technical academic and business writing, such as in science and engineering, use numerals for all numbers over ten, and use numerals for zero through nine when they refer to exact measurements (*2 litres, 1 hour*). (Technical usage does vary from discipline to discipline. Consult one of the style guides listed on pp. 142–43 for more details.)

Note Use a combination of numerals and words for round numbers over a million: *26 million, 2.45 billion.* And use either all figures or all words when several numbers appear together in a passage, even if convention would require a mixture.

34b. Commonly used numerals

In non-technical writing, numerals are conventional for certain information, even when the numbers could be spelled out in one or two words.

Days and years	Exact amounts of money
June 18, 1985 AD 12	$3.5 million $4.50
2002 456 BC	

Pages, chapters, volumes, acts, scenes, lines	Decimals, percentages, and fractions
Chapter 9, page 123	22.5 3½
Hamlet, Act 5, Scene 3	8% (*also* 48 percent or
Statistics, Volume 2	per cent)

Addresses	Scores and statistics
355 Clinton Avenue	a ratio of 8 to 1 21 to 7
Washington, DC 20036	

The time of day	
9:00 3:45	

34c. Beginnings of sentences

35

For clarity, spell out any number that begins a sentence. If the number requires more than two words, reword the sentence so that the number falls later and can be expressed as a numeral.

Faulty	*103* visitors asked for refunds.
Awkward	*One hundred and three* visitors asked for refunds.
Revised	Of the visitors, *103* asked for refunds.

35 Spelling

Sending a document out into the world with words misspelled is like going to a job interview without combing your hair or showing up at a formal wedding in jeans. It sends the wrong message to your readers. If you want them to read your document willingly and accurately, take time to verify your spelling with one of the many good Canadian dictionaries or computer word-processor spell-checkers available.

(35a.) British, American, or Canadian?

Canadian spelling used to follow British usage. Increasingly, however, Canadians are adopting American usage. Although it is usually acceptable (and very Canadian) to mix British and American spellings within one document, it is never acceptable to follow specific rules inconsistently.

For example, if you spell *theatre* with an *re* according to British spelling conventions, you should not then spell *metre* with an *er*, as in *meter*, which is American. Similarly, use both *colour* and *labour*, or *color* and *labor*, but not *colour* and *labor*. Many words that end in *re* and *our* in British spelling end in *er* and *or* in American spelling.

Be consistent as well with words that double their final *l*, that end in *ce* or *se*, or that end in *que*. Thus, *marvellous*, *defence*, and *cheque* are British (generally the preferred Canadian usage), while *marvelous*, *defense*, and *check* are American.

Some other words for which Canadians generally follow British spelling include *catalogue* (not *catalog*), *pyjamas* (not *pajamas*), and *whisky* (not *whiskey*).

It's best to decide on the appropriate usage for your audience and stick to it, either by consistently following one dictionary's preferences or by setting the preferences or your word processor's spell-checker preference. This book, for example, follows the preferences of *The Canadian Oxford Dictionary*.

(35b.) Using spell-checkers

Spell-checkers are useful for flagging possibly faulty spelling, but never automatically accept a spell-checker's advice. It will frequently highlight correctly spelled words while overlooking incorrect words such as homonyms. See sections 1k and 1l; as well, some HOMONYMS are listed in the Glossary of Usage.

VI Research and Documentation

36 Research Strategy

Writing a research essay is very much like writing any essay, except that your thesis is more likely to derive not primarily from your own ideas but from your careful analysis of source material from books, reference works, reports, periodicals, websites, and so on, that you have identified, located, evaluated, documented, criticized, and synthesized.

(36a) Topic, question, and thesis

As with any essay, focus and define your topic so that you care about the question and can manage the task within the assigned time and length.

Following the steps suggested in Chapter 1: The Writing Process, narrow and redefine your topic not as a tentative thesis *sentence* but as a *question* to be answered by further research:

What factors are responsible for reducing the East Coast cod stocks?

Is the Canadian health care system capable of handling outbreaks of new diseases like Severe Atypical Respiratory Syndrome (SARS)?

Do the separate cinematic traditions of Quebec and English Canada have any elements in common?

As your knowledge of your topic increases, you will revise your question. Eventually your answer to your research question will become your thesis.

37 Finding Sources

Depending on your research question or assigned task, you may consult a variety of sources. Many students are accustomed to gathering information from web-based sources, but instructors usually expect students to consult at least some academic print sources found in research libraries.

(37a.)   Kinds of sources

As much as possible you should rely on *primary sources*. These are first-hand accounts such as historical documents (letters, speeches, government documents, and so on), eyewitness testimony, works of literature, reports on experiments or surveys conducted by the writer, and your own interviews, experiments, observations, or correspondence.

In contrast, secondary sources report and analyze information drawn from other sources, often primary ones: a reporter's summary of a controversial issue, an historian's account of a battle, a critic's reading of a poem, a psychologist's evaluation of several studies. The most reliable secondary sources are published by academic or university presses and scholarly journals because, in order to be selected for publication, these sources must be vetted (peer-reviewed) by other experts in the scholarly field.

Secondary sources may contain helpful summaries and interpretations, as well as references to other sources, that direct, support, and extend your thinking. Most research-writing assignments, however, expect your own ideas to go beyond those you find in your sources.

(37b.)   Using a library

Begin with the Reference section, selecting the most specific reference work for your topic. Thus to learn about *The History of Emily Montague*, the first English novel written in Canada, use *The Oxford Companion to Canadian Literature* (specifically about Canadian literature) rather than *The Canadian Encyclopedia* (a general encyclopedia about Canada).

Use the library catalogue to locate other books and periodicals on your topic. Ask the Reference Librarian for assistance.

(37c.)   Periodical and essay indexes

Use special indexes (in print, CD-ROM, or online formats) such as the *Social Sciences Index* or the *Readers' Guide to Periodical Literature* to locate periodical material on your topic; use the *Essay and General Literature Index* to find essays and articles contained in books.

37d. Computer searches

Through CD-ROMs or online, search the catalogues of research libraries such as the Library of Congress or the British Library, and academic bibliographies such as the *MLA International Bibliography of Books and Articles on the Modern Languages and Literature*. Subscription databases like *ProQuest* and *EBSCO* allow you to access and download a précis or entire article from an academic journal.

Note Electronic searches require the right key words. Librarians can suggest helpful strategies.

37e. Locating internet sources

The internet can provide a wealth of material, including electronic mail, ListServs (email discussion groups), electronic publications, and the World Wide Web. Be careful, however, not to be overwhelmed by irrelevant information.

Search engines (software tools for locating information) like AltaVista or Google may generate a list of hundreds of sites for your topic. In that case, try limiting your search by using more keywords. Instead of *cinema* or *SARS*, try *Quebec cinema* or *SARS Toronto*. Since search engines proliferate and technology evolves, consult a librarian or other expert on how to use the search engines available to you.

37e

Note that web-based sources tend not to include material from before the 1980s. If you are researching a current scientific topic, you probably want the most up-to-date sources, but many topics in the arts and humanities require historical perspective, and you may want sources that are decades or centuries old.

Bookmark all websites you consult, but also record the bibliographic information, including date of access, that you will need to cite the source. (See appropriate documentation formats in Chapters 43–47).

38 Evaluating Sources

Research writing involves much more than finding sources and reporting their contents. The challenge and interest come from *selecting* appropriate sources and *interacting* with them through *critical reading*. Analyze the source, identifying its main ideas and assessing the quality of its evidence, bias, logic, and relevance. Evaluate its usefulness and quality, and relate its ideas to other texts and to your own ideas.

Sources that you locate in a research library have generally (but not inevitably) been previewed by publishers, scholars, and librarians. Although they still require evaluation, they will tend to be more trustworthy than online material you locate yourself.

38a. Evaluating print sources

To evaluate *relevance*, ask yourself:

- Does this source provide information, ideas, or analysis relevant to my topic?
- Is the source appropriately specialized?

To evaluate *reliability*, ask yourself:

- Is this source up to date?
- Is the author qualified to write on this topic?
- Does the author have any biases?
- Does the author appear to present information accurately and to assess it fairly?
- Do other reliable sources respect this source?

38b. Evaluating internet sources

Unlike scholarly books published by academic or university presses and scholarly articles published in academic journals, few websites are subject to peer review or editorial judgment. Many websites exist to promote particular commercial or political interests rather than to provide balanced views. Other websites may be created by people who know less about the topic than you do. Some websites contain errors of fact. Take extra care to assess the author of internet material for qualifications and bias and to evaluate the material critically. If in doubt, use only reliable electronic sources or databases maintained by governments, educational institutions, academic and professional associations and museums, or consult online editions of established newspapers and journals. Also consult websites that review other websites, such as *Internet Public Library* (*www.ipl.org/ref*) and *Librarians' Index to the Internet* (*http://lii.org*).

Check the electronic address

Website addresses (URLs) end with abbreviations that indicate what kind of organization sponsors the website: *edu* means an educational institution; *org* means a non-profit organization; *mil* means the military; and *com* means a commercial enterprise. Remember, however, that while a site ending in *edu* may originate in a university, it might be the personal web page of a biased or ill-informed individual. Even sites sponsored by governments or by non-profit organizations must be evaluated critically. Note that *ca* indicates a Canadian source.

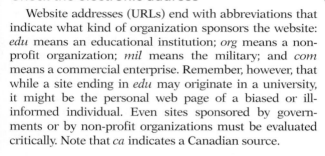

39 Taking Notes and Synthesizing Sources

39b

39a. Recording sources

Keep accurate records of the sources you consult. On cards or computer files, create a new bibliographic card or entry for every source you consult, and cross-reference all of your subject (content) notes from a source to the bibliographic card or entry for that source. Arrange bibliographic sources alphabetically by author's last name using an approved documentation style (see Chapters 44–47) as you compile your working bibliography. Note the library call number or website URL of each source so you can consult it again if necessary.

39b. Taking notes from sources

Take accurate notes. For each item of information or opinion, use a fresh note card (preferably a different size or colour from your bibliographic cards so you don't mix them up) or create a new computer file and back it up on diskettes. Label each note with a subject heading so you can arrange your notes by subject rather than by author or source. Indicate whether you are *paraphrasing*, *summarizing*, or *quoting* your source. (See Chapter 40: Summary, Paraphrase, Direct Quotation). Double-check exact quotations for accuracy, indicating any page breaks with a *slash* (section 28e), any changes or additions with *brackets* (28d), and any omissions with an *ellipsis* (28c). Then provide page references plus the author's last name or a similar brief cross-reference to your bibliography card or bibliographic file entry for this source. You can thus organize (and edit) your bibliographic information alphabetically by author while your notes can be shuffled and re-arranged by subject as you build your arguments.

On a computer, type notes accurately either into separate files (one per subject), as entries in a database, or continuously in one file with key word breakers indicating subject headings. Later use those key words with *Find* or *Search* commands to locate your notes for cutting and pasting into your draft.

(39c.) Synthesizing sources

39c

Record your reactions to your sources: Are the views insightful? Well supported? Provocative? Similar to other sources? Add your own comments, identified as such, to your notes as you engage in your research. Don't forget to write down any ideas that come to you as you read and record what others have said. Group similar sources together or cross-reference them. When your sources contradict one another, weigh their evidence and logic to arrive at your own analysis. Record your views: eventually, as you answer your research question, these views provide topic sentences for your paragraphs, to be supported by evidence from your sources. In this way your paragraphs will be organized around your own ideas and analysis, supporting your own thesis.

40 Summary, Paraphrase, Direct Quotation

Electronic sources can be downloaded and printed out in full, but, like photocopies of print sources or your own detailed notes, they still require your analysis and selection. It is thus a good idea to *summarize* or *paraphrase* your sources, although occasionally you will want to cite the exact words of a source as a direct quotation.

40a. Summary

When you SUMMARIZE, you condense an extended idea or argument into a sentence or more in your own words. Summary is most useful when you want to record the gist of an author's idea without the background or supporting evidence. Here, for example, is a passage summarized in a sentence:

Original quotation

The wealthy young men who enjoyed their socially-admired role as officers in the militia were quick to offer their services, displaying the leadership that was expected of the English-speaking, moneyed class who resided in "the Square Mile." One of the most notable among them was twenty-six-year-old Guy Melfort Drummond. Young Drummond, an officer in the 5th Royal Highlanders, seemed to have a glittering future. Handsome and very tall (six foot four), fluently bilingual and a millionaire, Drummond was being groomed for a career high in Conservative party politics, and there were those who whispered that the post of prime minister was not unlikely for Drummond some day.

—DANIEL D. DANCOCK, *Welcome to Flanders Fields*,
Toronto: M&S Paperback, 40.

Summary

Assuming the leadership roles expected of them, rich young men from the Montreal English-speaking establishment volunteered for war in 1914.

(40b.) Paraphrase

A PARAPHRASE follows much more closely the author's original presentation, but restated in your own words. Paraphrase is most useful when you want to reconstruct an author's line of reasoning or exposition, but don't feel the original words merit direct quotation. Here is a paraphrase of the final sentence in the passage quoted above:

Paraphrase

Tall, handsome, rich, and bilingual, Guy Drummond was thought by some to be a future Conservative prime minister.

Follow these guidelines when paraphrasing:

- Read the material until you understand it.
- Restate the main ideas in your own words using your own sentence structure.
- Be careful not to distort the author's meaning.

(40c.) Direct quotation

40c

If your purpose is to analyze the text of a particular work, such as a poem, historical document, or philosophical treatise, then you will use many direct quotations from the work. Otherwise you should quote from sources only in the following circumstances:

The author's original satisfies one of these requirements:

- The language is unusually eloquent or memorable.
- The quotation cannot be paraphrased without distortion.
- The words themselves are the subject of your discussion.
- The quotation represents the view of an important expert.
- The quotation is a graph, diagram, or table.
- The quotation is as short as possible.
- It includes only material relevant to your point.
- It is edited to eliminate examples and other unnecessary material (see note on p. 133).

When quoting from a source, copy the material exactly, including the original spelling, capitalization, and punctuation. Proofread every quotation at least twice when you copy it, and be sure to use quotation marks (Chapter 27) so that you won't later mistake the quotation for your own words. Indicate any page breaks with a slash (section 28e) so you will be able to cite the correct page if you end up using only a part of the quotation.

Note As long as you do not distort the original author's meaning and you use appropriate punctuation, you can make changes in quotations for clarity and concision. See Chapter 42: Integrating Sources into Your Text.

41 Avoiding Plagiarism

PLAGIARISM (from a Latin word for "kidnapper") is the presentation of someone else's ideas or words as your own. Whether deliberate or accidental, plagiarism is a serious and often punishable offence.

- *Deliberate* plagiarism includes copying a sentence from a source and passing it off as your own, summarizing someone else's ideas without acknowledging your debt, or buying a term paper and handing it in as your own.
- *Accidental* plagiarism includes forgetting to place quotation marks around another writer's words, omitting a source citation because you are not aware of the need for it, or carelessly copying a source when you mean to paraphrase.

Checklist for Avoiding Plagiarism

✓ What type of source are you using: your own independent material, common knowledge, or someone else's independent material? You must acknowledge someone else's material.

✓ If you are quoting someone else's material, is the quotation exact? Have you inserted quotation marks around quotations run into the text? Have you shown omissions with ellipsis marks and additions with brackets?

✓ If you are paraphrasing or summarizing someone else's material, have you used your own words and sentence structures, not the source author's? Does your paraphrase or summary employ quotation marks when you resort to the author's exact language? Have you represented the author's meaning without distortion?

41

✓ If you are using someone else's material in your own website, have you obtained any needed permission for your use? (See p. 136)

✓ Have you acknowledged every use of someone else's material in the place where you use it? Are all your source citations complete and accurate? (See pp. 134–35.)

✓ Does your list of works cited include all the sources you have drawn from in writing your paper? (See pp. 134–35.)

41a. What not to acknowledge

Your independent material

You are not required to acknowledge your own observations, thoughts, compilations of facts, or experimental results, expressed in your own words and format.

Common knowledge

You need not acknowledge common knowledge: the standard information of a field of study as well as folk literature and common-sense observations.

If you do not know a subject well enough to determine whether a piece of information is common knowledge, make a record of the source. As you read more about the subject, the information may come up repeatedly without acknowledgment, in which case it is probably common knowledge. But if you are still in doubt when you finish your research, always acknowledge the source.

41b. What *must* be acknowledged

You must always acknowledge other people's independent material—that is, any facts or ideas that are not common knowledge or your own. The source may be anything, including a book, an article, a movie, an interview, a microfilmed document, a computer program, a newsgroup posting, or an opinion expressed on the radio. You must acknowledge summaries or paraphrases of ideas or facts as well as quotations of the language and format in which ideas or facts appear:

wording, sentence structures, arrangement, and special graphics (such as a diagram). You must acknowledge another's material no matter how you use it, how much of it you use, or how often you use it.

Note See pp. 137–38 on integrating quotations into your own text without plagiarism. And see pp. 142–43 on acknowledging sources.

Copied language: Quotation marks and a source citation

The following example baldly plagiarizes the original quotation from Jessica Mitford's *Kind and Usual Punishment*, p. 9. Without quotation marks or a source citation, the example matches Mitford's wording (underlined) and closely parallels her sentence structure:

Original   The character and mentality of the keepers may be of more importance in understanding prisons than the character and mentality of the kept.

Plagiarism   But the character of prison officials (the keepers) is more important in understanding prisons than the character of prisoners (the kept).

To avoid plagiarism, the writer can paraphrase and cite the source (see the two revisions on p. 136) or use Mitford's actual words in quotation marks and with a source citation (here, in MLA style):

41b

Revision (quotation)   According to one critic of the penal system, "The character and mentality of the keepers may be of more importance in understanding prisons than the character and mentality of the kept" (Mitford 9).

Paraphrase or summary: Your own words and a source citation

The next example changes Mitford's sentence structure, but it still uses her words (underlined) without quotation marks and without a source citation:

Plagiarism   In understanding prisons, we should know more about the character and mentality of the keepers than of the kept.

To avoid plagiarism, the writer can use quotation marks and cite the source (see above) or *use his or her own words* and still *cite the source* (because the idea is Mitford's, not the writer's):

Revision   Mitford holds that we may be able to
(paraphrase)   learn more about prisons from the
                    psychology of the prison officials than
                    from that of the prisoners (9).

Revision   We may understand prisons better if
(paraphrase)   we focus on the personalities and atti-
                    tudes of the prison workers rather
                    than those of the inmates. (Mitford 9).

 Online sources

In general, you should acknowledge online sources
when you would any other source: whenever you use
someone else's independent material in any form. But online sources may present additional challenges as well:

- Keep in mind that online sources may change entirely. Be sure to record complete source information each time you consult the source. Without the
  source information, you *may not* use the source.
- A website may include links to other sites that are
  copyrighted in their own right and require your acknowledgment. The fact that one person has used a
  second person's work does not release you from the
  responsibility to acknowledge the second work.
- As a courtesy, you should obtain the author's permission to use any ideas, information, or wording
  you obtain from email correspondence or a discussion group.
- If you want to use material in something you pub-
  lish online, such as your own website, play it safe:
  seek permission from the copyright holder in addition to citing the source.
- Generally, you can find information about a site's
  copyright on the home page or at the bottoms of
  other pages: look for a notice using the symbol ©.
  Most worthwhile sites also provide information for
  contacting the author or sponsor. If you don't find a
  copyright notice, you *cannot* assume that the work
  is unprotected by copyright. Only if the site explicitly says it is not copyrighted or is available for free
  use can you use it online without permission.

41b

42 Integrating Sources into Your Text

The evidence of others' information and opinions should back up, not dominate, your own ideas. To synthesize evidence, you need to smooth the transitions between your ideas and words and those of your sources, and you need to give the reader a context for interpreting the borrowed material.

Note Integrating quotations into your text may involve several conventions discussed elsewhere:

- For guidelines on when to quote from sources, see pp. 132–33.
- For the punctuation of signal phrases such as *he insists,* see p. 139.
- For guidelines on when to run quotations into your text and when to display them separately from your text, see pp. 188–89.
- For the use of brackets ([ ]) to indicate changes in or additions to quotations, see p. 195.
- For the use of the ellipsis mark (…) to indicate omissions from quotations, see pp. 193–94.

42a. Introduction of borrowed material

42a

Integrate all quotations, paraphrases, and summaries smoothly into your own sentences, adding words as necessary to mesh structures.

Awkward	One editor disagrees with the view and "a good reporter does not fail to separate opinions from facts" (Lyman 52).
Revised	One editor disagrees with this view, <u>maintaining that</u> "a good reporter does not fail to separate opinions from facts" (Lyman 52).

To mesh your own and your source's words, you may sometimes need to make a substitution or addition to the quotation, signalling your change with brackets:

Words added	"The tabloids [of England] are a journalistic case study in bad reporting," claims Lyman (52).

Verb form changed	A bad reporter, Lyman implies, is one who "[fails] to separate opinions from facts" (52). [The bracketed verb replaces *fail* in the original.]
Capitalization changed	"[T]o separate opinions from facts" is a goal of good reporting (Lyman 52). [In the original, *to* is not capitalized.]
Noun supplied for pronoun	The reliability of a news organization "depends on [reporters'] trustworthiness," says Lyman (52). [The bracketed noun replaces *their* in the original.]

(42b.) Interpretation of borrowed material

Even when it does not conflict with your own sentence structure, borrowed material will be ineffective if you merely dump it in readers' laps without explaining how you intend it to be understood. In the following passage, we must figure out for ourselves that the writer's sentence and the quotation state opposite points of view.

| **Dumped** | Many news editors and reporters maintain that it is impossible to keep personal opinions from influencing the selection and presentation of facts. "True, news reporters, like everyone else, form impressions of what they see and hear. However, a good reporter does not fail to separate opinions from facts." (Lyman 52). |
| **Revised** | Many news editors and reporters maintain that it is impossible to keep personal opinions from influencing the selection and presentation of facts. <u>Yet not all authorities agree with this view. One editor grants that</u> "news reporters, like everyone else, form impressions of what they see and hear." But, he insists, "a good reporter does not fail to separate opinions from facts" (Lyman 52). |

Signal phrases

In the revised passage above, the words *One editor grants* and *he insists* are signal phrases: they tell readers who the source is and what to expect in the quotations. Signal phrases usually contain (1) the source author's name (or a substitute for it, such as *One editor* and *he*) and (2) a verb that indicates the source author's attitude or approach to what he or she says. In the passage above, *grants* implies concession and *insists* implies argument.

Below are some verbs to use in signal phrases. For the appropriate tense° of such verbs (present,° as here, or past° or past perfect°) see pp. 140–41.

Neutral	Infers or suggests	Argues	Uneasy or disparaging
comments	analyzes	claims	belittles
describes	asks	contends	bemoans
explains	assesses	defends	complains
illustrates	believes	disagrees	condemns
mentions	concludes	holds	deplores
notes	considers	insists	deprecates
observes	finds	maintains	derides
points out	predicts		laments
records	proposes	Agrees	warns
relates	reveals	accepts	
reports	shows	admits	
says	speculates	agrees	
sees	suggests	concedes	
thinks	supposes	concurs	
writes		grants	

Vary your signal phrases to suit your interpretation of borrowed material and also to keep readers' interest. A signal phrase may precede, interrupt, or follow the borrowed material:

Signal phrase precedes	<u>Lyman insists</u> that "a good reporter does not fail to separate opinions from facts" (52).
Signal phrase interrupts	"However," <u>Lyman insists</u>, "a good reporter does not fail to separate opinions from facts" (52).
Signal phrase follows	"[A] good reporter does not fail to separate opinions from facts," Lyman insists (52).

Background information

You can add information to a quotation to integrate it into your text and inform readers why you are using it. Often, you may want to provide the author's name in the text:

42b

Author named   Harold Lyman grants that "news reporters, like everyone else, form impressions of what they see and
hear." But, Lyman insists, "a good
reporter does not fail to separate
opinions from facts" (52).

If the source title contributes information about the
author or the context of the quotation, you can provide
it in the text:

Title given   Harold Lyman, in his book _The
Conscience of the Journalist_, grants
that "news reporters, like everyone
else, form impressions of what they
see and hear." But, Lyman insists,
"a good reporter does not fail to
separate opinions from facts" (52).

Finally, if the quoted author's background and experience reinforce or clarify the quotation, you can provide these credentials in the text:

Credentials   Harold Lyman, a newspaper editor
given   for more than 40 years, grants that
"news reporters, like everyone else,
form impressions of what they see
and hear." But, Lyman insists, "a
good reporter does not fail to separate opinions from facts" (52).

You need not name the author, source, or credentials in your text when you are simply establishing facts
or weaving together facts and opinions from varied
sources to support a larger point. In the following passage, the information is more important than the
source, so the name of the source is confined to a parenthetical acknowledgment:

The Christmas Truce of 1914 was the last expression of
traditional, conservative nineteenth-century values such
as honour, duty and sportsmanship (Eksteins 119–33).

(42c.) Discipline styles for integrating sources

In MLA style, generally use the PRESENT TENSE° when
discussing literary sources, since events in literature

happen *in the present* as we read:

> Throughout *The Wars*, Timothy Findley associates Robert Ross with animals. In the opening scene of the novel, for example, Robert is sitting "on his haunches" (1).

This parenthetical citation follows the Modern Language Association style (MLA), commonly used in literary studies (see Chapter 44).

Writers in history, art history, philosophy and related disciplines in the Humanities generally use either the PRESENT TENSE° or PRESENT PERFECT TENSE° of verbs in signal phrases:

> As Dancock has noted, "The wealthy young men who enjoyed their socially-admired role as officers in the militia were quick to offer their services, displaying the leadership that was expected of the English-speaking, moneyed class who resided in 'the Square Mile.'"[6]

The use of the raised (superscript) note number here follows the *Chicago Manual of Style* documentation style (CMS), commonly used in the Humanities (see Chapter 45).

Writers in the sciences generally use the PRESENT TENSE° for reporting results of a study (*The data suggest* . . .).

Otherwise use the PAST° or PAST PERFECT TENSE° in a signal phrase:

42a

> Lin (1999) has suggested that preschooling may significantly affect children's academic performance through high school (pp. 22–23).

The parenthetical citation here follows the American Psychological Association (APA) style, commonly used for social and life sciences (see Chapter 46). Another style for science writing is the Council of Biology Editors style (see Chapter 47.)

You need not name the author, source, or credentials in your text when you are simply establishing facts or weaving together facts and opinions from varied sources (although, of course, you must still acknowledge each source in a citation).

Note See pp. 88–91 and 93–95 for how to punctuate quotations. And see pp. 88–89 for when to display long quotations separately from your text.

43 Documenting Sources

Every time you borrow the words, facts, or ideas of others, you must document the source—that is, supply a reference (or document) telling readers that you borrowed the material and where you borrowed it from. (For guidelines on when sources must be documented, see Chapter 41.)

Editors and teachers in most academic disciplines require special documentation formats (or styles) in their scholarly journals and in students' papers. All the styles use a citation in the text that serves two purposes: it signals that material is borrowed, and it refers readers to detailed information about the source so that they can locate both the source and the place in the source where the borrowed material appears. The detailed source information appears either in footnotes or at the end of the paper.

Aside from these essential similarities, the disciplines' documentation styles differ markedly in citation form, arrangement of source information, and other particulars. Each discipline's style reflects the needs of its practitioners for certain kinds of information presented in certain ways—for instance, in-text citations in the social sciences indicate the date of the source's publication because currency is important.

43a. Documentation styles

This book details four documentation styles:

- MLA style, used in English, other modern languages, and some other humanities (Chapter 44)
- *Chicago Manual* style, used in history, art history, and some other disciplines (Chapter 45)
- APA style, used in psychology, educational psychology, and other social sciences (Chapter 46)
- CBE style, used in the biological and physical sciences and in mathematics (Chapter 47)

43b. Other styles

Some print or online guides to other documentation styles are

American Anthropological Association:
www.aaanet.org/pubs/style_guide.htm

American Chemical Society:
http://pubs.acs.org/books/references.shtml

American Institute of Physics:
www.aip.org/pubservs/style/4thed/toc.html

American Mathematical Society:
American Mathematical Society. *The AMS Author Handbook: General Instructions for Preparing Manuscripts*. Rev. ed. 1996.

American Medical Association:
Iverson, Cheryl (Ed.), et al. *American Medical Association Manual of Style: A Guide for Authors and Editors (AMA)*. 9th ed. 1997.

American Sociological Association:
www.asanet.org/pubs/pubs.html

Ask your instructor which style you should follow.

44 MLA Documentation Style

44a

Widely used in English, other modern languages, and other humanities, the MLA documentation style originates with the Modern Language Association. It appears in the *MLA Handbook for Writers of Research Papers,* sixth edition (2003), and the *MLA Style Manual and Guide to Scholarly Publishing,* second edition (1998). The MLA's website, at *www.mla.org/,* offers occasional updates and answers to frequently asked questions. In MLA style, brief parenthetical citations in the text (44a) direct readers to a list of works cited at the end of the text (44b).

44a. MLA parenthetical citations

Citation formats

The in-text citations of sources must include just enough information for the reader to locate (1) the appropriate source in your list of works cited and (2) the place in the source where the borrowed material appears. Usually, you can meet both these requirements by providing the author's last name and the page(s) in the source on which the borrowed material appears.

Note If the author is named in your text, you do not have to repeat the name in your parenthetical citation.

Index to MLA Parenthetical Citations

44a

1.   Author not named in your text

One researcher concludes that "women impose a distinctive construction on moral problems, seeing moral dilemmas in terms of conflicting responsibilities" (Gilligan 105).

2.   Author named in your text

One researcher, Carol Gilligan, concludes that "women impose a distinctive construction on moral problems, seeing moral dilemmas in terms of conflicting responsibilities" (105).

3.   A work with two or three authors

"Most historians," Copp and McAndrew observe, "in their preoccupation with weapons, tactics, technology, and grand strategy . . . have ignored the vast human dimension of battle" (11).

Historians have tended to ignore the psychological impact of battle (Copp and McAndrew 11).

4. A work with more than three authors

It took the combined forces of the Americans, Europeans, and Japanese to break the rebel siege of Beijing in 1900 (Lopez et al. 362).

Lopez, Salt, Ming, and Reisen observe that it took the combined forces of the Americans, Europeans, and Japanese to break the rebel siege of Beijing in 1900 (362).

5. A work with numbered paragraphs or screens instead of pages

According to Palfrey, twins raised apart report similar feelings (pars. 6–7).

6. An entire work (no page numbers)

Richard Brown's <u>Voyage of the Iceberg</u> tells the story of the iceberg that sank the <u>Titanic</u>.

<u>Voyage of the Iceberg</u> tells the story of the iceberg that sank the <u>Titanic</u> (Brown).

44a

7. A multi-volume work

After issuing the Emancipation Proclamation, Lincoln said, "What I did, I did after very full deliberations, and under a very heavy and solemn sense of responsibility" (5: 438).

If you name only one volume in your list of works cited, give only the page number in your text citation.

8. A work by an author of two or more cited works

An author's "<u>profession</u> of personal sincerity" may itself be a literary convention (Frye, <u>Fables</u> 45).

9. An unsigned work

One article notes that a death-row inmate may demand his own execution to achieve a fleeting notoriety ("Right").

10. A government document or a work with a corporate author

A 1996 report by Health Canada recommends limiting substances in private drinking water (6).

11. A source referred to by another source

George Davino maintains that "even small children have vivid ideas about nuclear energy" (qtd. in Boyd 22).

12. A literary work

For novels that may be available in many editions, cite part, chapter, or other numbers as well as page number.

Toward the end of James's novel, Maggie suddenly feels "the intimate, the immediate, the familiar, as she hadn't had them for so long" (535; pt. 6, ch. 41).

Later in <u>King Lear</u> Shakespeare has the disguised Edgar say, "The prince of darkness is a gentleman" (3.4.147).

The citation above lists act number, scene number, and line number, respectively.

44a

13. The Bible

Abbreviate any book title longer than four letters, then give chapter and verse(s):

According to the Bible, at Babel God "did . . . confound the language of all the earth" (Gen. 11.9).

14. More than one work

Two recent articles point out that a computer badly used can be less efficient than no computer at all (Gough and Hall 201; Richards 162).

15. An electronic source

Most electronic sources can be cited just as printed sources are. For a source with no named author, see model 9. For a source that uses paragraph or some other numbers instead of page numbers, see model 5. For a source with no numbering, just give the author's name, either in parentheses or in the text, as in model 6:

Michael Tourville, for one, believes that Europe's new single currency will quickly strengthen the continent's large and technologically advanced companies.

Footnotes or endnotes in special circumstances

Footnotes or endnotes may supplement parenthetical citations when you cite several sources at once, when you comment on a source, or when you provide information that does not fit easily in the text. Signal a footnote or endnote in your text with a numeral raised above the appropriate line. Then write a note with the same numeral.

Text   At least five subsequent studies have confirmed these results.[1]

Note   [1] Abbott and Winger 266–68; Casner 27; Hoyenga 78–79; Marino 36; Tripp, Tripp, and Walk 179–83.

If the note appears as a footnote, place it at the bottom of the page on which the citation appears, set it off from the text with quadruple spacing, and single-space the note itself. If the note appears as an endnote, place it in numerical order with the other endnotes on a page between the text and the list of works cited; double-space all the endnotes.

44b

44b. MLA list of works cited

At the end of your paper, a list titled "Works Cited" includes all the sources you quoted, paraphrased, or summarized in your paper. The format of the list's first page is illustrated below. Arrange your sources in alphabetical order by the last name of the author (the first author if there is more than one). If an author is not given in the source, alphabetize the source by the first main word of the title (excluding *A, An,* or *The*). In the models that follow for various sources, note these main features:

• Double-space all entries. Type the first line of each entry at the left margin, and indent all subsequent lines one-half inch or five spaces.

- List the author's name last-name first. If there are two or more authors, list all names after the first in normal order. Separate the names with commas.
- Give full titles, capitalizing all important words (see p. 115). (For periodical titles, omit any *A, An,* or *The.*) Underline the titles of books and periodicals; place titles of periodical articles in quotation marks.
- Provide publication information after the title. For books, give place of publication, publisher's name, and date. (Shorten publishers' names—for instance, *Little* for Little, Brown and *Carleton UP* for Carleton University Press.) For periodical articles, give the volume or issue number, date, and page numbers.
- Separate the main parts of an entry with periods followed by one space.

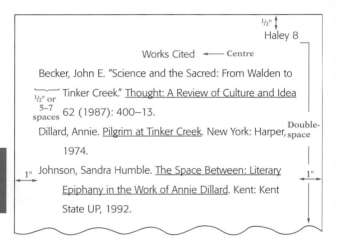

44b

Books

1.   A book with one author

Gilligan, Carol. <u>In a Different Voice: Psychological Theory and</u>
<u>Women's Development</u>. Cambridge: Harvard UP, 1982.

2.   A book with two or three authors

Mitchell, Claudia, and Jacqueline Reid-Walsh. <u>Childspaces: Researching</u>
<u>Children's Popular Culture</u>. London: Routledge, 2002.

3.   A book with more than three authors

Lopez, Geraldo, et al. <u>China and the West</u>. Boston: Little, 1990.

Lopez, Geraldo, Judith P. Salt, Anne Ming, and Henry Reisen. <u>China</u>
<u>and the West</u>. Boston: Little, 1990.

4.   Two or more works by the same author(s)

Frye, Northrop. <u>The Double Vision: Language and Meaning in</u>
<u>Religion</u>. Toronto: U of Toronto P, 1991.

———. <u>Fables of Identity: Studies in Poetic Mythology</u>. New York:
Harcourt, 1963.

5.   A book with an editor

Ruitenbeek, Hendrick, ed. <u>Freud as We Knew Him</u>. Detroit: Wayne
State UP, 1973.

6.   A book with an author and an editor

Burney, Frances. <u>Evelina, or, The History of a Young Lady's Entrance</u>
<u>into the World</u>. Ed. Stewart J. Cooke. Norton Critical Edition.
New York: Norton, 1998.

7.   A translation

Marchessault, Jovette. <u>Mother of the Grass</u>. Trans. Yvonne M. Klein.
Vancouver: Talon, 1989.

8.   A book with a corporate author

Lorenz, Inc. <u>Research in Social Studies Teaching</u>. Baltimore: Arrow,
2002.

9.   A familiar reference work

<u>Gage Canadian Dictionary</u>. Toronto: Gage, 1998 ed.

10. An anonymous book

<u>The Dorling Kindersley World Reference Atlas</u>. London: Dorling,
2000.

11. A later edition

Bollinger, Dwight L. <u>Aspects of Language</u>. 2nd ed. New York:
Harcourt, 1975.

12. A republished book

James, Henry. <u>The Golden Bowl</u>. 1904. London: Penguin, 1966.

44b

Index to MLA Works-Cited Models

44b

13. A book with a title in its title

Eco, Umberto. <u>Postscript to</u> The Name of the Rose. Trans. William
Weaver. New York: Harcourt, 1983.

14. A work in more than one volume

Lincoln, Abraham. <u>The Collected Works of Abraham Lincoln</u>. Ed. Roy
P. Basler. 8 vols. New Brunswick: Rutgers UP, 1953.

Lincoln, Abraham. <u>The Collected Works of Abraham Lincoln</u>. Ed. Roy
P. Basler. Vol. 5. New Brunswick: Rutgers UP, 1953. 8 vols.

44b

15. A work in a series

Bergman, Ingmar. <u>The Seventh Seal</u>. Modern Film Scripts Series. New
York: Simon, 1968.

16. An anthology

Barnet, Sylvan, et al., eds. <u>An Introduction to Literature</u>. 12th ed. New
York: Longman, 2001.

17. A selection from an anthology or collection

Duer, Leslie. "Portraits, Effigies, and the Narrative Impulse." <u>Literature
and Ethics: Essays Presented to A. E. Malloch</u>. Ed. Gary Wihl and
David Williams. Montreal: McGill-Queen's UP, 1988. 32–45.

18. Two or more selections from the same anthology

Harrison, Keith. "Other Tricks." Thompson 97.

Shields, Carol. "The Journal." Thompson 91–94.

Thompson, Kent, ed. <u>Open Windows: Canadian Short Stories</u>.
Kingston: Quarry, 1988.

19. An introduction, preface, foreword, or afterword

Adamson, Judith. Introduction. <u>Reflections</u>. By Graham Greene.
Toronto: Lester, 1990. ix–xvii.

20. An article in a reference work

"Mammoth." <u>The Columbia Encyclopedia</u>. 1993.

Mark, Herman F. "Polymers." <u>The New Encyclopaedia Britannica:</u>
<u>Macropaedia</u>. 16th ed. 1991.

Periodicals: Journals, magazines, newspapers

21. A signed article in a journal with continuous pagination throughout the annual volume

Grundy, Isobel. "Books and the Woman: An Eighteenth-Century Owner
and Her Libraries." <u>English Studies in Canada</u> 20 (1994): 1–20.

22. A signed article in a journal that pages issues separately or that numbers only issues, not volumes

Dacey, June. "Management Participation in Corporate Buy-Outs."
<u>Management Perspectives</u> 7.4 (2001): 20–31.

23. A signed article in a monthly or bimonthly magazine

Stein, Harry. "Living with Lies." <u>Esquire</u> Dec. 1981: 23.

24. A signed article in a weekly or biweekly magazine

Hawaleshka, Danylo. "Killer Viruses." <u>Maclean's</u> 31 Mar. 2003: 50–51.

25. A signed article in a daily newspaper

Lopez-Pacheco, Alexandra. "Health Lessons Start at Home." <u>National Post</u> 11 Aug. 2003: SR6.

26. An unsigned article

"The Right to Die." <u>Time</u> 11 Oct. 1976: 101.

27. An editorial or letter to the editor

"Does Watching Count?" Editorial. <u>Globe and Mail</u> 21 Aug. 2003: A16.

Dowding, Michael. Letter. <u>Economist</u> 5–11 Jan. 1985: 4.

28. A review

Dunne, John Gregory. "The Secret of Danny Santiago." Rev. of <u>Famous All over Town</u>, by Danny Santiago. <u>New York Review of Books</u> 16 Aug. 1984: 17–27.

29. An abstract of a dissertation

Steciw, Steven K. "Alterations to the Pessac Project of Le Corbusier." Diss. U of Cambridge, England, 1986. <u>DAI</u> 46 (1986): 565C.

44b

30. An abstract of an article

Lever, Jane. "Sex Differences in the Games Children Play." <u>Social Problems</u> 23 (1976): 478–87. <u>Psychological Abstracts</u> 63 (1976): item 1431.

Electronic sources

Electronic sources include those available on CD-ROM, diskette, or magnetic tape and those available online, as through the internet. Conventions for citing electronic sources are still evolving. Check the MLA website (*www.mla.org/*) for the latest formats.

Note Online sources require two special pieces of information:

• Give the date when you consulted the source as well as the date when the source was posted online. The posting date comes first, with other publication information. Your access date falls near the end of the entry, just before the electronic address.

- Give the source's exact and complete electronic address, enclosed in angle brackets (< >). Place the address at the end of the entry. If you must break an address from one line to the next, do so *only* after a slash, and do not hyphenate.

Try to locate all of the information required, but if you have searched and cannot find something, then give what you can find.

31. A source on CD-ROM or diskette

CD-ROM periodical also published in print:

Ramirez, Anthony. "Computer Groups Plan Standards." <u>New York</u>

 <u>Times</u> 14 Dec. 1993, late ed.: D5. <u>New York Times Ondisc</u>.

 CD-ROM. UMI-Proquest. June 1994.

CD-ROM periodical not published in print:

"Vanguard Forecasts." <u>Business Outlook</u>. CD-ROM. Information

 Access. March 2002.

Non-periodical CD-ROM, diskette, or tape:

Shelley, Mary Wollstonecraft. <u>Frankenstein</u>. <u>Classic Library</u>. CD-ROM.

 Alameda: Andromeda, 1993.

44b

32. Electronic mail or an online posting

Electronic mail:

Millon, Michele. "Re: Grief Therapy." Email to the author. 4 May 2003.

An email discussion list:

Tourville, Michael. "European Currency Reform." Online posting. 6

 Jan. 2003. International Finance Discussion List. 23 Feb. 2003

 <http://www.weg.isu.edu/finance-dl/>.

If archived, cite the Archive and its URL in place of the List and its URL.

A newsgroup:

Cramer, Sherry. "Recent Investment Practices." Online posting. 26

 Mar. 2003. 3 Apr. 2003 <news:biz.investment.current.2700>.

33. A home page for a course

Begin with the instructor's name (last name first); then the course title; then a description such as *Course home page* (do not underline or use quotation marks for title or description); then the course dates; then the department name, followed by the institution, the access date, and the URL:

Lambrinos, Alicia. Introduction to College English. Course home page.

   January–May 2003. English Department, Marianopolis

   College. 16 April 2003 <http://www2.marianopolis.edu/

   faculty/lambrinos.html>.

34. An online scholarly project, reference database, or personal or professional site

A scholarly project or database:

<u>Scots Teaching and Research Network</u>. Ed. John Corbett. 2 Feb.

   2001. U of Glasgow. 5 Mar. 2001

   <http://www.arts.gla.ac.uk/www/english/comet/ starn.htm>.

A short work within a scholarly project:

Barbour, John. "The Brus." <u>Scots Teaching and Research Network</u>. Ed.

   John Corbett. 2 Feb. 2003. U of Glasgow. 5 Mar. 2003

   <http://www.arts.gla.ac.uk/www/english/comet/starn/

   poetry/brus/contents.htm>.

A book within a scholarly project:

Austen, Jane. <u>Emma</u>. Ed. Ronald Blythe. Harmondsworth: Penguin,

   1972. <u>Oxford Text Archive</u>. 1994. Oxford U. 15 Dec. 2001

   <ftp://ota.ox.ac.uk/pub/ota/public/english/Austen/

   emma.1519>.

A personal or professional site:

Lederman, Leon. <u>Topics in Modern Physics—Lederman</u>. 12 Dec.

   2002 <http://www-ed.fnal.gov/samplers/hsphys/people/

   lederman.html>.

35. An online book

James, Henry. <u>The Turn of the Screw</u>. New York: Scribner's, 1908–09.

   4 Mar. 1998 <http://www.americanliterature.com/TS/

   TSINDX.HTML>.

36. An article in an online periodical

An article in a scholarly journal:

Palfrey, Andrew. "Choice of Mates in Identical Twins." <u>Modern
Psychology</u> 4.1 (1996): 12 pars. 25 Feb. 1996
<http://www.liasu.edu/modpsy/palfrey4(1).htm>.

An article in a newspaper:

Rusk, James. "Pearson Drug Ring Broken." <u>globe and mail.com</u> 22
Aug. 2004 <http://www.globeandmail.com/servlet/story/
RTGAM.20030821.udrug0822/BNStory/National/>.

An article in a magazine:

Palevitz, Barry A., and Ricki Lewis. "Death Raises Safety Issues for
Primate Handlers." <u>Scientist</u> 2 Mar. 1998: 1+. 27 Mar. 1998
<http://www.the-scientist.library.upenn.edu/yr1998/mar/
palevitz_pl_980302.html>.

37. An online review

Detwiler, Donald S., and Chu Shao-Kang. Rev. of <u>Important
Documents of the Republic of China</u>, ed. Tan Quon Chin.
<u>Journal of Military History</u> 56.4 (1992): 669–84. 16 Sept.
1997 <http://www.jstor.otg/fcgi-bin/jstor/viewitem.fcg/
08993718/ 96p0008x>.

38. A work from an online subscription service

Wilkins, Johanna M. "The Myths of the Only Child." <u>Psychology Update</u>
11:1 (1999): 16–20. <u>ProQuest Health and Medical Complete</u>.
ProQuest Direct. Manhattan Community College Lib., New
York. 20 Dec. 2001 <http://www.umi.com/proquest/>.

39. An online graphic, video, or audio file

Hamilton, Calvin J. "Components of Comets." Diagram. <u>Space Art</u>.
1997. 20 December 2001 <wysisyg://94/http://
spaceart.com/solar/eng/comet.htm>.

44b

40. A synchronous communication (MUD, MOO, etc.)

Bruckman, Amy. MediaMOO Symposium: Virtual Worlds for

Business? 20 Jan. 2002. MediaMOO. 26 Feb. 2002

<http://www.cc.gatech.edu/Amy.Bruckman/MediaMOO/

cscw-symposium-98.html>.

41. Computer software

Project Scheduler 9000. Ver. 4.1. Orlando: Scitor, 2002.

Other sources

42. A government document

United States. Cong. House. Committee on Ways and Means.

Medicare Payment for Outpatient Physical and Occupational

Therapy Services. 102nd Cong., 1st sess. Washington: GPO,

1991.

43. A musical composition or work of art

Mozart, Wolfgang Amadeus. Piano Concerto no. 20 in D Minor, K. 466.

If citing a published reproduction of an art work, include the source:

44b

Thomson, Tom. Snow in October. National Gallery of Canada, Ottawa.

The Group of Seven and Tom Thomson: An Introduction. By

Anne Newlands. Willowdale ON: Firefly, 1995. 31.

44. A film or video recording

Spielberg, Steven, dir. Schindler's List. Perf. Liam Neeson and Ben

Kingsley. Universal, 1993.

Serenade. Chor. George Balanchine. Perf. San Francisco Ballet. Dir.

Hilary Beane. 1981. Videocassette. PBS Video, 1987.

45. A television or radio program

Kenyon, Jane, and Donald Hall. "A Life Together." Bill Moyers' Journal.

PBS. WNET, New York. 17 Dec. 1998.

46. A performance

<u>The English Only Restaurant</u>. By Silvio Martinez Palau. Dir. Susana
Tubert. Puerto Rican Traveling Theater, New York. 27 July 1990.

Lamon, Jeanne, cond. Tafelmusik Baroque Orch. Concert. Trinity-St.
Paul's Centre, Toronto. 17 Sept. 2003.

47. A recording

Mitchell, Joni. <u>For the Roses</u>. Asylum, 1972.

Brahms, Johannes. Concerto no. 2 in B-flat, op. 83. Perf. Artur
Rubinstein. Cond. Eugene Ormandy. Philadelphia Orch. RCA,
1999.

48. A letter

Buttolph, Mrs. Laura E. Letter to Rev. and Mrs. C. C. Jones. 20 June
1857. In <u>The Children of Pride: A True Story of Georgia and
the Civil War</u>. Ed. Robert Manson Myers. New Haven: Yale UP,
1972. 334.

Packer, Ann E. Letter to the author. 15 June 2002.

49. A lecture or address

Khouri, Katia. "Ownership Convergence." Symposium on Canadian
Journalism. City of Cambridge. Cambridge City Hall, 16 Oct.
2002.

50. An interview

Graaf, Vera. Personal interview. 19 Dec. 2001.

Martin, William. Interview. "Give Me That Big Time Religion." <u>Frontline</u>.
PBS. WGBH, Boston. 13 Feb. 1984.

44b

45 *Chicago Manual* Documentation Style

In history, art history, and many other disciplines, writers rely on *The Chicago Manual of Style*, 14th edition (1993), or the student reference adapted from it, *A Manual for Writers of Term Papers, Theses, and Dissertations*, by Kate L. Turabian, 6th edition revised by John Grossman and Alice Bennett (1996). Both books detail two documentation styles. One, used mainly by scientists and social scientists, closely resembles the style of the American Psychological Association, covered in the next chapter. The other style, used more in the humanities, calls for footnotes or endnotes and a bibliography. The Chicago Manual has a website that answers frequently asked questions about Chicago style: *www.press.uchicago.edu/Misc/Chicago/cmosfaq.html*.

(45a.) *Chicago Manual* endnotes or footnotes and works-cited entries

In the *Chicago Manual* note style, a raised numeral in the text refers the reader to source information in endnotes or footnotes. (Ask your instructor what kind of note you should use. The first citation of a source provides complete information about the source.) At the end of the paper, a list titled "Works Cited" includes all sources in alphabetical order.

45a

Whether providing footnotes or endnotes, use single spacing for each note and double spacing between notes. With footnotes, separate the notes from the text with a short line, as shown in the following sample:

In 1901, Madras, Bengal, and Punjab were a few of the huge Indian provinces governed by the British viceroy.[6] British rule, observes Stuart Cary Welch, "seemed as permanent as Mount Everest."[7]

5 spaces

      6. Martin Gilbert, *Atlas of British History* (New York: Dorset Press, 1968), 96.

Single-space

Double-space

      7. Stuart Cary Welch, *India: Art and Culture* (New York: Metropolitan Museum of Art, 1985), 421.

Single-space

1"

For the list of sources at the end of the paper, use the format below. Arrange the sources alphabetically by the authors' last names.

Notes and works-cited entries differ in key ways:

Note

6. Martin Gilbert, *Atlas of British History* (New York: Dorset Press, 1968), 96.

Works cited

Gilbert, Martin. *Atlas of British History*. New York: Dorset Press, 1968.

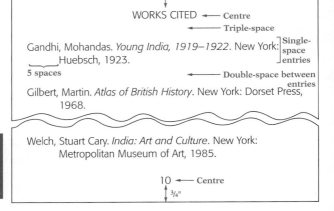

- In the note, start with a number (typed on the line and followed by a period) that corresponds to the note number in the text. In the works-cited entry, omit any starting number.
- In the note, indent the first line five spaces. In the works-cited entry, indent the second and subsequent lines five spaces.
- In the note, give the author's name in normal order. In the works-cited entry, begin with the author's last name.
- In the note, use commas between elements such as author's name and title. In the works-cited entry, use periods between elements, followed by one space.
- In the note, enclose publication information in parentheses, with no preceding punctuation. In the works-cited entry, precede the publication information with a period and don't use parentheses.
- In the note, include the specific page number(s) you borrow from, omitting *p.* or *pp.* In the works-cited

entry, which cites the entire source, omit page numbers except for entire parts of books or articles in periodicals.

Notes and works-cited entries also share certain features:

- Underline or italicize the titles of books and periodicals (ask your instructor for his or her preference).
- Enclose in quotation marks the titles of parts of books or articles in periodicals.
- Do not abbreviate publishers' names, but omit *Inc.*, *Co.*, and similar abbreviations.
- Do not use *p.* or *pp.* before page numbers.

(45b.) *Chicago Manual* models

In the following models for common sources, notes and works-cited entries appear together for easy reference. Be sure to use the numbered note form for notes and the unnumbered works-cited form for works-cited entries.

Books

1.   A book with one, two, or three authors

     1. Carol Gilligan, *In a Different Voice: Psychological Theory and Women's Development* (Cambridge: Harvard University Press, 1982), 27.

Gilligan, Carol. *In a Different Voice: Psychological Theory and Women's Development*. Cambridge: Harvard University Press, 1982.

     1. Bernard J. Frieden and Lynne B. Sagalyn, *Downtown, Inc: How America Rebuilds Cities* (Cambridge: MIT Press, 1989), 16.

Frieden, Bernard J., and Lynne B. Sagalyn. *Downtown, Inc.: How America Rebuilds Cities*. Cambridge: MIT Press, 1989.

2.   A book with more than three authors

     2. Joan Stryker and others, eds., *Encyclopedia of American Life*, 2d ed. (Boston: Winship, 1995), 126–28.

Stryker, Joan, William Hones, William Parker, and Sylvia Mannes, eds. *Encyclopedia of American Life*. 2d ed. Boston: Winship, 1995.

3.   A book with an editor

     3. Hendrick Ruitenbeek, ed., *Freud as We Knew Him* (Detroit: Wayne State University Press, 1973), 64.

Ruitenbeek, Hendrick, ed. *Freud as We Knew Him*. Detroit: Wayne State University Press, 1973.

45b

45b

4.   A book with an author and an editor

4. Frances Burney, *Evelina, or, The History of a Young Lady's Entrance into the World*, ed. Stewart J. Cooke (New York: Norton, 1998), 137.

Burney, Frances. *Evelina, or, The History of a Young Lady's Entrance into the World*. Edited by Stewart J. Cooke. New York: Norton, 1998.

5.   An anonymous work

5. *Gage Canadian Dictionary* (Toronto: Gage, 1998).

Gage Canadian Dictionary. Toronto: Gage, 1998.

6.   A later edition

6. Dwight L. Bollinger, *Aspects of Language*, 2d ed. (New York: Harcourt Brace Jovanovich, 1975), 20.

Bollinger, Dwight L. *Aspects of Language*. 2d ed. New York: Harcourt Brace Jovanovich, 1975.

7.   A work in more than one volume

7. Abraham Lincoln, *The Collected Works of Abraham Lincoln*, ed. Roy P. Basler (New Brunswick: Rutgers University Press, 1953), 5:426–28.

Lincoln, Abraham. *The Collected Works of Abraham Lincoln*. Ed. Roy P. Basler. Vol. 5. New Brunswick: Rutgers University Press, 1953.

8.   A selection from an anthology

8. Leslie Duer, "Portraits, Effigies, and the Narrative Impulse," in *Literature and Ethics: Essays Presented to A. E. Malloch*, ed. Gary Wihl and David Williams (Montreal: McGill-Queen's University Press, 1988), 37.

Duer, Leslie. "Portraits, Effigies, and the Narrative Impulse." In *Literature and Ethics: Essays Presented to A. E. Malloch*, ed. Gary Wihl and David Williams, 32–45. Montreal: McGill-Queen's University Press, 1988.

Periodicals: Journals, magazines, newspapers

9.   An article in a journal with continuous pagination throughout the annual volume

9. Isobel Grundy, "Books and the Woman: An Eighteenth-Century Owner and Her Libraries," *English Studies in Canada* 20 (1994): 11.

Grundy, Isobel. "Books and the Woman: An Eighteenth-Century Owner and Her Libraries." *English Studies in Canada* 20 (1994): 1–20.

10. An article in a journal that pages issues separately

10. June Dacey, "Management Participation in Corporate Buy-Outs," *Management Perspectives* 7, no. 4 (1994): 22.

Dacey, June. "Management Participation in Corporate Buy-Outs." *Management Perspectives* 7, no. 4 (1994): 20–31.

11. An article in a popular magazine

11. Mark Stevens, "Low and Behold," *New Republic*, 24 December 1990, 28.

Stevens, Mark. "Low and Behold." *New Republic*, 24 December 1990, 27–33.

12. An article in a newspaper

12. Alexandra Lopez-Pacheco, "Health Lessons Start at Home," *National Post*, 11 August 2003, SR6.

Lopez-Pacheco, Alexandra. "Health Lessons Start at Home." *National Post*, 11 August 2003, SR6.

Electronic sources

The 15th edition of *The Chicago Manual of Style* offers expanded models for documenting electronic sources. Consult *www.chicagomanualofstyle.org*.

Note Follow MLA style when you must break an electronic address in a note or works-cited entry: break only after a slash, and do not hyphenate.

13. A source on a periodical CD-ROM

A source also published in print:

13. Peter H. Lewis, "Many Updates Cause Profitable Confusion," *New York Times*, 21 January 1999, national ed., D5. *New York Times Ondisc* [CD-ROM], UMI-ProQuest, March 1999.

Lewis, Peter H. "Many Updates Cause Profitable Confusion." *New York Times*, 21 January 1999, national ed., D1, D5. *New York Times Ondisc* [CD-ROM]. UMI-ProQuest, March 1999.

A source not published in print:

45b

13. "Vanguard Forecasts," *Business Outlook* [CD-ROM], Information Access, March 2002.

"Vanguard Forecasts." *Business Outlook* [CD-ROM]. Information Access, March 2002.

14. A source on a non-periodical CD-ROM

14. Mary Wollstonecraft Shelley, *Frankenstein*, Classic Library [CD-ROM] (Alameda, Calif.: Andromeda, 1993).

Shelley, Mary Wollstonecraft. *Frankenstein*. Classic Library [CD-ROM]. Alameda, Calif.: Andromeda, 1993.

15. An online book

15. Jane Austen, *Emma* [book online], ed. Ronald Blythe (Harmondsworth, Eng.: Penguin, 1972, accessed 15 December 1998), *Oxford Text Archive*; available from ftp://ota.ox.ac.uk/public/english/Austen/emma.1519; Internet.

Austen, Jane. *Emma* [book online]. Edited by Ronald Blythe. Harmondsworth, Eng.: Penguin, 1972. Accessed 15 December 1998. *Oxford Text Archive*. Available from ftp://ota.ox.ac.uk/public/english/Austen/emma.1519; Internet.

16. An article in an online periodical

16. Andrew Palfrey, "Choice of Mates in Identical Twins," *Modern Psychology* 4, no. 1 (1996): par. 10 [journal online]; available from http://www.liasu.edu/modpsy/palfrey4(1)htm; Internet; accessed 25 February 2001.

Palfrey, Andrew. "Choice of Mates in Identical Twins." *Modern Psychology* 4. no. 1 (1996): 12 pars. [journal online]. Available from http://www.liasu.edu/modpsy/ palfrey4(1).htm; Internet. Accessed 25 February 2001.

17. An online database

17. *Scots Teaching and Research Network* [database online], ed. John Corbett (Glasgow: University of Glasgow, 2 February 1998, accessed 5 March 2002); available from http://www.arts.gla.ac.uk/www/comet/starn.htm; Internet.

Scots Teaching and Research Network [database online]. Edited by John Corbett. Glasgow: University of Glasgow, 2 February 1998. Accessed 5 March 2002. Available from http://www.arts.gla.ac.uk/www/comet/starn.htm; Internet.

Other sources

18. A government document

18. B.C., Ministry of Community, Aboriginal and Women's Services, *A Guide to Aboriginal Organizations and Services in British Columbia* (Victoria: Queen's Printer, 2000), 56.

B.C. Ministry of Community, Aboriginal and Women's Services. *A Guide to Aboriginal Organizations and Services in British Columbia.* Victoria: Queen's Printer, 2000.

45b

19. A work of art

19. Tom Thomson, *Snow in October*, oil, c. 1915, National Gallery of Canada, Ottawa.

Thomson, Tom. *Snow in October*, oil, c. 1915. National Gallery of Canada, Ottawa.

20. Two or more citations of the same source

Reference to the same source cited in the preceding note:

8. Janet Lever, "Sex Differences in the Games Children Play," *Social Problems* 23 (1976): 482.

9. Ibid., 483.

Reference to a source cited earlier than the preceding note:

1. Carol Gilligan, *In a Different Voice: Psychological Theory and Women's Development* (Cambridge: Harvard University Press, 1982), 27.

2. Carol Gilligan, "Moral Development in the College Years," *The Modern American College*, ed. A. Chickering (San Francisco: Jossey-Bass, 1981), 286.

3. Gilligan, *In a Different Voice*, 47.

Omit the shortened title if you are using only one source by the cited author(s).

46 APA Documentation Style

The documentation style of the American Psychological Association is used in psychology and some other social sciences and is very similar to the styles in sociology, economics, and other disciplines. The following adapts the APA style from the *Publication Manual of the American Psychological Association*, 5th edition (2001). The APA provides occasional updates of its style and answers to FAQs at *www.apastyle.org/faqs.html*.

46a

46a. APA parenthetical citations

Citation formats

In the APA style, parenthetical citations in the text refer to a list of sources at the end of the text. The basic parenthetical citation contains the author's last name, the date of publication, and the page number or identifying number from which material is borrowed, unless none is available. The APA also recommends an identifying number for a paraphrase.

1. Author not named in your text

One critic of Milgram's experiments insisted that the subjects "should have been fully informed of the possible effects on them" (Baumrind, 1968, p. 34).

2.   Author named in your text

Baumrind (1968) insisted that the subjects in Milgram's study "should have been fully informed of the possible effects on them" (p. 34).

3.   A work with two authors

Pepinsky and DeStefano (1997) demonstrate that a teacher's language often reveals hidden biases.

One study (Pepinsky & DeStefano, 1997) demonstrates hidden biases in a teacher's language.

46a

4.   A work with three to five authors
First reference:

Pepinsky, Dunn, Rentl, and Corson (1993) further demonstrate the biases evident in gestures.

Later references:

In the work of Pepinsky et al. (1993), the loaded gestures include head shakes and eye contact.

5.   A work with six or more authors

One study (Rutter et al., 1996) attempts to explain these geographical differences in adolescent experience.

6. A work with a corporate author

An earlier prediction was even more sombre (Lorenz Research, 1997).

7. An anonymous work

One article ("Right to Die," 1976) noted that a death-row inmate may crave notoriety.

8. One of two or more works by the same author(s)

At about age seven, most children begin to use appropriate gestures to reinforce their stories (Gardner, 1973a).

(See the reference for this source on p. 172.)

9. Two or more works by different authors

Two studies (Herskowitz, 1994; Marconi & Hamblen, 1990) found that periodic safety instruction can dramatically reduce employees' accidents.

10. A source referred to by another source

46a

Supporting data appear in a study by Wong (cited in Marconi & Hamblen, 1990).

11. An electronic source

Electronic sources can be cited like printed sources, usually with the author's last name and the publication date. When quoting or paraphrasing electronic sources that number paragraphs instead of pages, provide the paragraph number preceded by the symbol "¶" if you have it, or by "para."

Ferguson and Hawkins (1998) did not anticipate the "evident hostility" of participants (¶ 6).

Footnotes for supplementary content

When you need to explain something in your text—for instance, commenting on a source or providing data that don't fit into the relevant paragraph—you may place the supplementary information in a footnote. Follow the instructions for footnotes in the *Chicago Manual* style (pp. 159–66). Be careful not to overuse such notes: they can be more distracting than helpful.

46b. APA reference list

In APA style, the in-text parenthetical citations refer to the list of sources at the end of the text. In this list, titled "References," you include full publication information on every source cited in your paper. The reference list falls at the end of the paper, numbered in sequence with the preceding pages. The sample below shows the elements and their spacing.

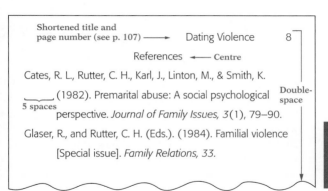

Prepare APA references as follows:

• Arrange the sources alphabetically by the author's last name or, if there is no author, by the first main word of the title.
• Double-space all entries.
• Type the first line of each entry at the left margin, and indent all subsequent lines one-half inch or five to seven spaces. (This so-called hanging indent is clearest for student papers. For manuscripts that will be published, the APA specifies an indention for the first line and not the others.)
• For works with up to six authors, list all authors last-name first, separating names and parts of names with commas. Use initials for first and middle names. Use an ampersand (&) rather than *and* before the last author's name. See model 3 (p. 172) for treatment of seven or more authors.

Index to APA References

46b

- Place the date of publication in parentheses after the author's or authors' names, followed by a period. Generally this date is year only, although for sources like newspaper and magazine articles, it includes month and sometimes day as well.
- In titles of books and articles, capitalize only the first word of the title, the first word of the subtitle, and proper names; all other words begin with small letters. In titles of journals, capitalize all significant words.
- Italicize the titles of books and periodicals, along with any comma or period following. Do not italicize or use quotation marks around the titles of periodical articles.
- For print sources that are not periodicals (such as books or government documents), give the city of publication. Unless the city is easily identifiable (such as Toronto, Halifax, New York, Chicago) add a comma after the city's name and give the postal abbreviation for the province or state (Sherbrooke, QC) followed by a colon. If the city is easily identifiable,

46b

follow it by a colon. If the name of the publisher
identifies the province or state (University of Alberta
Press) you may eliminate the reference to the
province or state.

- For non-periodical print sources, give the publisher's
  name after the place of publication and a colon. Use
  shortened names for many publishers (such as "Morrow" for "William Morrow") and omit "Co.," "Inc.,"
  and "Publishers." Give full names for associations, corporations, and university presses, however, and do not
  omit "Books" or "Press" from the publisher's name.

- Use the abbreviation *p.* or *pp.* before page numbers
  in books and newspapers, but *not* in other periodicals. For inclusive page numbers, include all figures:
  667–668.

- Separate the parts of the reference (author, date, title, and publication information) with a period and
  one space. Do not use a final period in references to
  electronic sources, which conclude with an electronic address.

Books

1.   A book with one author

Rodriguez, R. (1982). *A hunger of memory: The education of Richard Rodriguez.* Boston: Godine.

2.   A book with two to six authors

Nesselroade, J. R., & Baltes, P. B. (1979). *Longitudinal research in the study of behavioral development.* New York: Academic.

3.   A book with seven or more authors

Wimple, P. B., Van Eijk, M., Potts, C. A., Hayes, J. Obergau, W. R., Zimmer, S., et al. (2001). *Case studies in moral decision making among adolescents*. San Francisco: Jossey-Bass.

4.   A book with an editor

Dohrenwend, B. S., & Dohrenwend, B. P. (Eds.). (1974). *Stressful life events: Their nature and effects.* New York: Wiley.

5.   A book with a translator

Trajan, P. D. (1927). *Psychology of animals.* (H. Simone, Trans.). Washington, DC: Halperin.

6.   A book with a corporate author

Lorenz, Inc. (1992). *Research in social studies teaching.* Baltimore: Arrow.

7.   An anonymous book

Merriam-Webster's collegiate dictionary (10th ed.). (1993). Springfield, MA: Merriam-Webster.

8.   Two or more works by the same author(s) published in the same year

Gardner, H. (1973a). *The arts and human development.* New York: Wiley.

46b

Gardner, H. (1973b). *The quest for mind: Piaget, Lévi-Strauss, and the structuralist movement.* New York: Knopf.

9.   A later edition

Bollinger, D. L. (1975). *Aspects of language* (2nd ed.). New York: Harcourt Brace Jovanovich.

10. A work in more than one volume

Lincoln, A. (1953). *The collected works of Abraham Lincoln* (R. P. Basler, Ed.). (Vol. 5). New Brunswick, NJ: Rutgers University Press.

Lincoln, A. (1953). *The collected works of Abraham Lincoln* (R. P. Basler, Ed.). (Vols. 1–8). New Brunswick, NJ: Rutgers University Press.

11. An article or chapter in an edited book

Paykel, E. S. (1974). Life stress and psychiatric disorder: Applications of the clinical approach. In B. S. Dohrenwend & B. P. Dohrenwend (Eds.), *Stressful life events: Their nature and effects* (pp. 239–264). New York: Wiley.

Periodicals: journals, magazines, newspapers

46b

12. An article in a journal with continuous pagination throughout the annual volume

Emery, R. E. (1982). Marital turmoil: Interpersonal conflict and the children of discord and divorce. *Psychological Bulletin, 92,* 310–330.

13. An article in a journal that pages issues separately

Dacey, J. (1994). Management participation in corporate buy-outs. *Management Perspectives, 7*(4), 20–31.

14. An abstract of a journal article

Emery, R. E. (1982). Marital turmoil: Interpersonal conflict and the children of discord and divorce. *Psychological Bulletin*, 92,

310–330. Abstract obtained from Psychological Abstracts,

1992, 69, Item 1320.

15. An article in a magazine

Auletta, K. (2001, January 15). Final offer. *The New Yorker*, 40–46.

16. An article in a newspaper

Kolata, G. (2001, January 7). Kill all the bacteria! *The New York

Times*, pp. B1, B3.

17. An unsigned article

The right to die. (1976, October 11). *Time*, 121, 101.

18. A review

Dinnage, R. (1987, November 29). Against the master and his men

[Review of the book *A mind of her own: The life of Karen

Horney*]. *The New York Times Book Review*, 10–11.

Electronic sources

In general, the APA's electronic-source references begin as those for print references do: author(s), date, title. Then you add information on when and how you
retrieved the source. For example, an online source
might conclude *Retrieved August 6, 2001, from
http://sites.unc.edu/~daniel/social_constructionism/* (in
APA style, no period follows an electronic address at
the end of the reference). When you need to divide an
electronic address from one line to the next, APA style
calls for breaking *only* after a slash or before a period.
Do not hyphenate an electronic address.

Try to locate all the information required by a model, referring to page 136 for help. However, if you
search for and still cannot find some information, then
give what you can find. If a source has no publication
date, use "n.d." (for *no date*) in place of a publication
date (see model 28, p. 176).

19. A journal article published online and in print

Palfrey, A. (1996). Choice of mates in identical twins [Electronic ver-

sion]. *Modern Psychology*, 4(1), 26–40.

20. An article in an online journal

Wissink, J. A. (2000). Techniques of smoking cessation among teens
and adults. *Adolescent Medicine,* 2. Retrieved August 16,
2001, from http://www.easu.edu/AdolescentMedicine/
2-Wissink. html

21. A journal article from an electronic database

Wilkins, J. M. (1999). The myths of the only child. *Psychology
Update,* 11(1), 16–23. Retrieved December 20, 1999, from
ProQuest Direct database.

22. An abstract from an electronic database

Wilkins, J. M. (1999). The myths of the only child. *Psychology
Update,* 11(1), 16–23. Abstract retrieved December 20,
1999, from ProQuest Direct database.

23. An article in an online newspaper

Pear, R. (2001, January 23). Gains reported for children of welfare to
work families. *The New York Times on the Web.* Retrieved
January 23, 2001, from http://www.nytimes.com/2001/01/
23/national/232/WELF.html

46b

24. An entire website (text citation)

The APA's website provides answers to frequently asked questions
about style (http://www.apa.org).

Cite an entire website (rather than a specific page or
document) by giving the electronic address in your text.

25. An independent document on the web

Anderson, D. (2001, May 1). *Social constructionism and MOOs.*
Retrieved August 6, 2001, from http://sites.unc.edu/~daniel/
social_constructionism/

26. A document from the website of a university or
government agency

McConnell, L. M., Koenig, B. A., Greely, H. T., & Raffin, T. A. (2001,
August 17). *Genetic testing and Alzheimer disease. Has the*

time come? Retrieved September 1, 2001, from Stanford
University, Project in Genomics, Ethics, and Society website:
http://scbe.stanford.edu/pges

27. An online government report

U.S. Department of Commerce. National Telecommunications and
Information Administration. (1999, July). *Falling through the
net: Defining the digital divide*. Retrieved April 12, 2001, from
http://www.ntia.doc.gov/ntiahome/digitaldivide/

28. A multi-page online document

Elston, C. (n.d.). *Multiple intelligences*. Retrieved June 6, 2001, from
http://education.com/teachspace/intelligences/

29. A part of an online document

Elston, C. (n.d.). Logical/math intelligence. In *Multiple intelligences*.
Retrieved June 6, 2001, from http://education.com/teach-
space/intelligences/logical.jsp

30. A retrievable online posting

Tourville, M. (2001, January 6). European currency reform. Message
posted to International Finance electronic mailing list, archived
at http://www.liasu.edu/finance-dl/46732

Include postings to discussion lists and newsgroups in
your list of references only if they are retrievable by
others. The source above is archived (as the reference
makes plain) and thus retrievable at the address given.

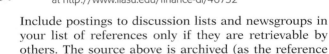

31. Electronic mail or a non-retrievable online posting (text citation)

At least one member of the research team has expressed reserva-
tions about the design of the study (L. Kogod, personal communication, February 6, 2000).

Personal electronic mail and other online postings that
are not retrievable by others should be cited only in
your text, as in the example above.

32. Computer software

Project scheduler 9000 [Computer software]. (2001). Orlando, FL: Scitor.

Other Sources

33. A report

Gerald, K. (1958). *Micro-moral problems in obstetric care* (Report No. NP-71). St. Louis: Catholic Hospital Association.

Jolson, M. K. (1981). *Music education for preschoolers* (Report No. TC-622). New York: Teachers College, Columbia University. (ERIC Document Reproduction Service No. ED 264 488)

34. A government publication

Ontario. Ministry of Citizenship. Office for Disability Issues. (1992). *Word Choices: A Lexicon of Preferred Terms for Disability Issues.* Toronto: Author.

Stiller, A. (1996). *Historic preservation and tax incentives.* Washington, DC: U.S. Department of the Interior.

Canada. Parliament. Senate. Standing Committee on Social Affairs, Science and Technology. Subcommittee on Veterans Affairs. (1998, March 19). *Proceedings, 9.* 35th Parl., 1st Sess., 1998–99. Ottawa: Public Works and Government Services Canada.

46b

35. An abstract of a dissertation

Steciw, S. K. (1986). Alterations to the Pessac project of Le Corbusier. *Dissertation Abstracts International, 46*, 565C. (UMI No. 2164877)

Delaune, M. L. (2001). *Child care in single-mother and single-father families: Differences in time, activity, and stress.* Unpublished doctoral dissertation, University of California, Davis.

36. A published interview

Brisick. W. C. (1998, July 1). [Interview with Ishmael Reed]. *Publishers Weekly,* 41–42.

For an interview you conduct yourself, use an in-text parenthetical citation.

37. A motion picture

Cite films beginning with the title, unless you are emphasizing an individual's contribution:

Spielberg, S. (Director). (1993). *Schindler's list* [Motion picture]. United States: Viacom.

American Psychological Association (Producer). (2001). *Ethnocultural psychotherapy* [Motion picture]. (Available from the American Psychologial Association, 7509 First Street, NE, Washington, DC 20002-4343, or online from http://www.apa.org/videos/4310240.html).

38. A musical recording

Rogers, G. (2002). Night drive. *All that is* [CD]. St. Paul, MN: Red House Records.

39. A television series or episode

Taylor, C., Cleveland, R., & Andries, L. (Producers). (2001). *Six feet under* [Television series]. New York: HBO.

Cleveland, R. (Writer), & Engler, M. (Director). (2001). Dillon Michael Cooper [Television series episode]. In C. Taylor, R. Cleveland, & L. Andries (Producers), *Six feet under.* New York: HBO.

47 CSE Documentation Style

Writers in the life sciences, physical sciences, and mathematics rely for documentation style on *Scientific Style and Format: The CBE Style Manual for Authors, Editors, and Publishers*, 6th edition (1994).[1] (The former Council of Biology Editors, or CBE, is now known

---

[1]Revisions for the 7th edition of this style manual were under way when this book went to press. For more information, visit the CSE website at www.councilscienceeditors.org.

as The Council of Science Editors.) This book details two documentation styles: one very close to APA style, using authors' names and publication dates in parenthetical text citations (see the previous chapter); and one using in-text numbers to refer to a list of numbered references that are sequenced in order of their citation in the text. The latter style is discussed below. Ask your instructor which style you should use.

(47a.) CSE numbered text citations

In the following examples of CSE in-text citations, the numbers refer to a numbered list of references at the end of the paper:

Two standard references[1,2] use this term.

These forms of immunity have been extensively researched.[3]

According to one report,[4] research into some forms of viral immunity is almost non-existent.

Hepburn and Tatin[2] do not discuss this project.

- Within the text, use a raised number or numbers to refer to numbered sources in the reference list at the end of the text.
- The number for each source is based on the order in which you cite the source in the text: the first cited source is 1, the second is 2, and so on.
- When you cite a source you have already cited and numbered, use the original number again (see the last example above, which reuses the number 2 from the first example). This reuse is the key difference between the CSE numbered citations and numbered references to footnotes or endnotes (pp. 159–61). In the CSE style, each source has only one number, determined by the order in which the source is first cited. With notes, in contrast, the numbering proceeds in sequence, so that sources have as many numbers as they have citations in the text.
- When you cite two or more sources at once, arrange their numbers in sequence and separate them with a comma and no space, as in the first example above.

47b

(47b.) CSE numbered references

Begin the list of sources for the CSE style at the end of the text, numbering the pages in sequence with the

text pages. Use the page format given for APA references on p. 169 (but you may omit the shortened title
before the page number). For the references themselves, follow these guidelines:

- Title the list of sources "References."
- Single-space the entries, and double-space between entries.
- Arrange the entries in numerical order—that is, in order of their citation in the text, *not* alphabetically.
- Begin each entry on a new line and number it. Type the number on the line of type (not raised), and follow it with a period and a space. Indent subsequent lines of each entry directly under the first word of the first line.
- List authors' names with the last name first, fol-lowed by initials for first and middle names. Do not use a comma after the last name or periods or space with the initials.
- Separate authors' names with commas.
- Do not underline or use quotation marks for any titles.
- In journal titles, capitalize all significant words. In book and article titles, capitalize only the first word and any proper nouns.
- For books, separate the name of the publisher from the date of publication with a semicolon and a space. End the reference with the total number of pages in the book, followed by *p.*
- For a journal article, put the date of publication im-mediately after the title of the journal, followed by the volume number and the inclusive page numbers for the article (with duplicated digits omitted): "Science 1990; 256:212–6." For a journal that pages each issue separately, add the month (and day, if relevant) after the year, and add the issue number in unspaced parentheses after the volume number: "1996 3 Mar;16(8):16." For all journals, use no punctuation be-tween title and date of publication. Put an unspaced semicolon between the date and volume number. Put an unspaced colon between the volume number (or parenthetical issue number) and the inclusive pages (see the examples above and models 6–7).

Books

1.   A book with one author

1.   Gould SJ. Time's arrow, time's cycle. Cambridge: Harvard Univ Pr; 1987. 222 p.

2.   A book with more than one author

2.   Hepburn PX, Tatin JM. Human physiology. New York: Columbia Univ Pr; 1975. 1026 p.

3.   A book with an editor

3.   Jonson P, editor. Anatomy yearbook. Los Angeles: Anatco; 1987. 628 p.

4.   A selection from a book

4.   Krigel R, Laubenstein L, Muggia F. Kaposi's sarcoma. In: Ebbeson P, Biggar RS, Melbye M, editors. AIDS: a basic guide for clinicians. Philadelphia: WB Saunders; 1987. p 100–26.

47b

5.   An anonymous work

5.   [Anonymous]. Health care for multiple sclerosis. New York: US Health Care; 1992. 86 p.

Periodicals: Journals, magazines, newspapers

6.   An article in a journal with continuous pagination throughout the annual volume

6.   Ancino R, Carter KV, Elwin DJ. Factors contributing to viral immunity: a review of the research. Developmental Biology 1983;30:156–9.

7.   An article in a journal that pages issues separately

7.   Milbank Symposium. Medical decision making for the dying. Milbank Quarterly 1986 Feb;64(2):26–40.

8. An article in a newspaper

8.   Krauthammer C. Lifeboat ethics: the case of Baby Jesse. Washington Post 1986 June 13;Sect A:33(col 1).

9. An article in a magazine

9.   Van Gelder L. Countdown to motherhood: when should you have a baby? Ms. 1986 Dec:37–39.

Other sources

10. A government document

10.   Health Canada. Guidelines for Canadian Drinking Water Quality. Ottawa, ON: Government of Canada, 1996. 90 p.

11.   House (US). Medicare payment for outpatient occupational therapy services. 102nd Cong., 1st Sess. House Doc. nr 409; 1991.

11. An electronic source

12.   Project scheduler 8000 [computer program]. Version 3.1. Orlando (FL): Scitor; 1995. 1 computer disk: 3 1[[fracsl]]2 in. Accompanied by: 1 manual. System requirements: IBM PC or fully compatible computer; DOS 5.0 or higher; 320K RAM; hard disk with a minimum of 2 MB of free space.

13.   Grady GF. The here and now of hepatitis B immunization. Today's Medicine [serial online] 1993 May 2;Doc nr 2:[2620 words]. Available from: Public Access Computer Systems Forum PACS-L via Internet. Accessed 1996 Jan 21.

Websites for Writing and Research

In addition to *The Little, Brown Handbook* website at **www.ablongman.com/littlebrown**, a number of other sites provide help for researchers and writers. Check out the following sites, but remember that websites and URLs change frequently.

Purdue Online Writing Lab is a searchable collection of over 130 handouts on most of the topics covered by this book. **http://owl.english.purdue.edu/index.html**

The Elements of Style, William Strunk and E. B. White's classic guide to clear writing, is available on line. **www.bartleby.com/141**

HyperGrammar is a University of Ottawa site that provides especially strong help with grammar, punctuation, and exercises for ESL students. **www.uottawa.ca/academic/arts/writcent/hypergrammar**

Writing Across the Curriculum is a Malaspina College site for research and writing. **www.mala.bc.ca/www/wac/wac.htm**

Writing in the Disciplines is a University College of the Cariboo site on academic and professional writing. **www.cariboo.bc.ca./disciplines/**

WWW

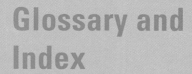

Glossary and Index

Glossary of Usage

This glossary provides notes on words or phrases that often cause problems for writers. The recommendations for standard written English are based on current dictionaries and usage guides. Items labelled NON-STANDARD should be avoided in final drafts of academic and business writing. Those labelled COLLOQUIAL and SLANG appear in some informal writing and may occasionally be used for effect in more formal academic and career writing. (Words and phrases labelled COLLOQUIAL include those labelled IN-FORMAL by many dictionaries.) See Chapter 6 for more on levels of language.

a, an Use *a* before words beginning with consonant sounds: *a historian, a one-o'clock class, a university.* Use *an* before words that begin with vowel sounds, including silent *h*'s: *an orgy, an L, an honour.*

The article before an abbreviation depends on how the abbreviation is read: *She has an NSRC grant. (NSRC is read as one word beginning with the vowel sound "en.") He is writing an SAT exam tomorrow. (SAT is read as three separate letters beginning with the vowel sound "ess.")*

See also pp. 65–67 on the uses of *a/an* versus *the.*

accept, except *Accept* is a verb° meaning "receive." *Except* is usually a preposition° or conjunction° meaning "but for" or "other than"; when it is used as a verb, it means "leave out." *I can accept all your suggestions except the last one. I'm sorry you excepted my last suggestion from your list.*

advice, advise *Advice* is a noun,° and *advise* is a verb:° *Take my advice; do as I advise you.*

affect, effect Usually *affect* is a verb,° meaning "to influence," and *effect* is a noun, meaning "result": *The drug did not affect his driving; in fact, it seemed to have no effect at all.* But *effect* occasionally is used as a verb meaning "to bring about": *Her efforts effected a change.* And *affect* is used in psychology as a noun meaning "feeling or emotion": *One can infer much about affect from behaviour.*

all ready, already *All ready* means "completely prepared," and *already* means "by now" or "before now": *We were all ready to go to the movie, but it had already started.*

all right *All right* is always two words. *Alright* is a common misspelling.

all together, altogether *All together* means "in unison," or "gathered in one place." *Altogether* means "entirely." *It's*

USAGE

not <u>altogether</u> true that our family never spends vacations <u>all together</u>.

allusion, illusion An *allusion* is an indirect reference, and an *illusion* is a deceptive appearance: *Paul's constant <u>allusions</u> to Shakespeare created the <u>illusion</u> that he was an intellectual.*

a lot *A lot* is always two words, used informally to mean "many." *Alot* is a common misspelling.

among, between In general, use *between* only for relationships of two and *among* for more than two.

amount, number Use *amount* with a singular noun that names something not countable (a non-count noun°): *The <u>amount</u> of <u>food</u> varies.* Use *number* with a plural noun that names more than one of something countable (a count noun°): *The <u>number</u> of <u>calories</u> must stay the same.*

and/or *And/or* indicates three options: one or the other or both (*The decision is made by the mayor <u>and/or</u> the council*). If you mean all three options, *and/or* is appropriate. Otherwise, use *and* if you mean both, *or* if you mean either.

anxious, eager *Anxious* means "nervous" or "worried" and is usually followed by *about*. *Eager* means "looking forward" and is usually followed by *to*. *I've been <u>anxious</u> about getting blisters. I'm <u>eager</u> (not <u>anxious</u>) <u>to</u> get new cross-training shoes.*

anybody, any body; anyone, any one *Anybody* and *anyone* are indefinite pronouns;° *any body* is a noun° modified by *any; any one* is a pronoun° or adjective° modified by *any. How can <u>anybody</u> communicate with <u>any body</u> of government? Can <u>anyone</u> help Amy? She has more work than <u>any one</u> person can handle.*

any more, anymore *Any more* means "no more"; *anymore* means "now." Both are used in negative constructions: *He doesn't want <u>any more</u>. She doesn't live here <u>anymore</u>.*

anyways, anywheres Non-standard for *anyway* and *anywhere*.

are, is Use *are* with a plural subject° (*books <u>are</u>*), *is* with a singular subject (*book <u>is</u>*). See p. 52.

as Substituting for *because, since,* or *while, as* may be vague or ambiguous: *<u>As</u> we were stopping to rest, we decided to eat lunch.* (Does *as* mean "while" or "because"?) *As* never should be used as a substitute for *whether* or *who. I'm not sure <u>whether</u> (not <u>as</u>) we can make it. That's the man <u>who</u> (not <u>as</u>) gave me directions.*

as, like See *like, as*.

at this point in time Wordy for *now, at this point,* or *at this time*.

awful, awfully Strictly speaking, *awful* means "awe-inspiring." As intensifiers meaning "very" or "extremely" (*He tried awfully hard*), *awful* and *awfully* should be avoided in formal speech or writing.

a while, awhile *Awhile* is an adverb;° *a while* is an article° and a noun.° *I will be gone awhile* (not *a while*). *I will be gone for a while* (not *awhile*).

bad, badly In formal speech and writing, *bad* should be used only as an adjective;° the adverb° is *badly*. *He felt bad because his tooth ached badly*. In *He felt bad,* the verb *felt* is a linking verb° and the adjective *bad* modifies the subject° *he,* not the verb *felt*.

being as, being that Colloquial for *because,* the preferable word in formal speech or writing: *Because* (not *Being as*) *the world is round, Columbus never did fall off the edge*.

beside, besides *Beside* is a preposition° meaning "next to." *Besides* is a preposition meaning "except" or "in addition to" as well as an adverb° meaning "in addition." *Besides, several other people besides you want to sit beside Dr. Christensen*.

between, among See *among, between*.

bring, take Use *bring* only for movement from a farther place to a nearer one and *take* for any other movement. *First, take these books to the library for renewal, then take them to Mr. Daniels. Bring them back to me when he's finished*.

can, may Strictly, *can* indicates capacity or ability, and *may* indicates permission: *If I may talk with you a moment, I believe I can solve your problem*.

chōse, choose The verb *choose* describes action in the present while *chose* (pronounced with a long o) refers to action in the past: *Please choose one. I chose mine yesterday*.

climatic, climactic *Climatic* comes from *climate* and refers to weather: *Last winter's temperatures may indicate a climatic change. Climactic* comes from *climax* and refers to a dramatic high point: *During the climactic duel between Hamlet and Laertes, Gertrude drinks poisoned wine*.

complement, compliment To *complement* something is to add to, complete, or reinforce it: *Her yellow blouse complemented her black hair*. To *compliment* something is to make a flattering remark about it: *He complimented her on her hair. Complimentary* can also mean "free": *complimentary tickets*.

conscience, conscious *Conscience* is a noun° meaning "a sense of right and wrong"; *conscious* is an adjective° meaning "aware" or "awake." *Though I was barely conscious, my conscience nagged me*.

continual, continuous *Continual* means "constantly recurring": *Most movies on television are continually interrupted* *by commercials. Continuous* means "unceasing": *Some cable channels present movies <u>continuously</u> without commercials.*

could of See *have, of.*

criteria The plural of *criterion* (meaning "standard for judgment"): *Our <u>criteria</u> are strict. The most important <u>criterion</u> is a sense of humour.*

data The plural of *datum* (meaning "fact"). Though *data* is often used as a singular noun, most careful writers still treat it as plural: *The data <u>fail</u>* (not *<u>fails</u>*) *to support the hypothesis.*

device, devise *Device* is the noun,° and *devise* is the verb:° *Can you <u>devise</u> some <u>device</u> for getting his attention?*

different from, different than *Different from* is preferred: *His purpose is <u>different from</u> mine.* But *different than* is widely accepted when a construction using *from* would be wordy: *I'm a different person now <u>than</u> I used to be* is preferable to *I'm a different person now <u>from the person</u> I used to be.*

disinterested, uninterested *Disinterested* means "impartial": *We chose Pete, as a <u>disinterested</u> third party, to decide who was right. Uninterested* means "bored" or "lacking interest": *Unfortunately, Pete was completely <u>uninterested</u> in the question.*

don't *Don't* is the contraction for *do not,* not for *does not: I <u>don't</u> care, you <u>don't</u> care,* and *he <u>doesn't</u>* (not *<u>don't</u>*) *care.*

due to *Due to* is always acceptable after a verb to refer back to the subject:° *His grey hairs were <u>due to</u> age.* Many object to *due to* meaning "because of" (*<u>Due to</u> the holiday, class was cancelled*). A rule of thumb is that *due to* is always correct after a form of the verb *be* but questionable otherwise.

eager, anxious See *anxious, eager.*

effect See *affect, effect.*

elicit, illicit *Elicit* is a verb° meaning "bring out" or "call forth." *Illicit* is an adjective° meaning "unlawful." *The crime <u>elicited</u> an outcry against <u>illicit</u> drugs.*

enthused Sometimes used colloquially as an adjective° meaning "showing enthusiasm." The preferred adjective is *enthusiastic: The coach was <u>enthusiastic</u>* (not *<u>enthused</u>*) *about the team's victory.*

etc. *Etc.,* the Latin abbreviation for "and other things," should be avoided in formal writing and should not be used to refer to people. When used, it should not substitute for precision, as in *The government provides health care, <u>etc.,</u>* and it should not end a list beginning *such as* or *for example.*

everybody, every body; everyone, every one *Everybody* and *everyone* are indefinite pronouns:° *<u>Everybody</u>* (*<u>everyone</u>*) *knows Tom steals. Every one* is a pronoun° modified by *every,* and *every body* a noun° modified by *every.* Both refer to each thing or person of a specific group and are typically followed by *of*: *Every body of water in the province has been tested, so everybody can swim safely this summer.*

everyday, every day *Everyday* is an adjective° meaning "used daily" or "common"; *every day* is a noun° modified by *every*: *Everyday problems tend to arise every day.*

everywheres Non-standard for *everywhere*.

except See *accept, except*.

explicit, implicit *Explicit* means "stated outright": *I left explicit instructions. Implicit* means "implied, unstated": *We had an implicit understanding.*

farther, further *Farther* refers to additional distance (*How much farther is it to the beach?*), and *further* refers to additional time, amount, or other abstract matters (*I don't want to discuss this any further*).

feel Avoid this word in place of *think* or *believe: She thinks* (not *feels*) *that the law should be changed.*

fewer, less *Fewer* refers to individual countable items (a plural noun°), *less* to general amounts (a singular noun): *Skim milk has fewer calories than whole milk. We have less milk left than I thought.*

further See *farther, further*.

get *Get* is easy to overuse; watch out for it in expressions such as *it's getting better* (substitute *improving*), *we got done* (substitute *finished*), and *the mayor has got to* (substitute *must*).

good, well *Good* is an adjective,° and *well* is nearly always an adverb:° *Larry's a good dancer. He and Linda dance well together. Well* is properly used as an adjective only to refer to health: *You look well.* (*You look good,* in contrast, means "Your appearance is pleasing.")

hanged, hung Though both are past-tense forms° of *hang, hanged* is used to refer to executions and *hung* is used for all other meanings: *Louis Riel was hanged* (not *hung*). *I hung* (not *hanged*) *the picture you gave me.*

have, of Use *have,* not *of,* after helping verbs° such as *could, should, would, may,* and *might: You should have* (not *should of*) *told me.*

he, she; he/she Convention has allowed the use of *he* to mean "he or she," but most writers today consider this usage inaccurate and unfair because it excludes females. The construction *he/she,* one substitute for *he,* is awkward and objectionable to most readers. The better choice is to use *he or she,* to recast the sentence in the plural, or to rephrase. For instance: *After the infant learns to creep, he or* *she progresses to crawling. After infants learn to creep, they progress to crawling. After learning to creep, the infant progresses to crawling.* See also pp. 29–31 and 59.

herself, himself See *myself, herself, himself, yourself.*

hisself Non-standard for *himself.*

hopefully *Hopefully* means "with hope": *Freddy waited hopefully.* The use of *hopefully* to mean "it is to be hoped," "I hope," or "let's hope" is now very common; but since many readers continue to object strongly to the usage, you should avoid it. *I hope* (not *Hopefully*) *Eliza will be here soon.*

if, whether For clarity, use *whether* rather than *if* when you are expressing an alternative: *If I laugh hard, people can't tell whether I'm crying.*

illicit See *elicit, illicit.*

illusion See *allusion, illusion.*

implicit See *explicit, implicit.*

imply, infer Writers or speakers *imply,* meaning "suggest": *Jim's letter implies he's having a good time.* Readers or listeners *infer,* meaning "conclude": *From Jim's letter I infer he's having a good time.*

irregardless Non-standard for *regardless.*

is, are See *are, is.*

is when, is where These are faulty constructions in sentences that define: *Adolescence is a stage* (not *is when a person is*) *between childhood and adulthood. Socialism is a system in which* (not *is where*) *government owns the means of production.*

its, it's *Its* is the pronoun° *it* in the possessive case:° *That plant is losing its leaves. It's* is a contraction for *it is: It's likely to die if you don't water it.*

kind of, sort of, type of In formal speech and writing, avoid using *kind of* or *sort of* to mean "somewhat": *He was rather* (not *kind of*) *tall.*

 Kind, sort, and *type* are singular: *This kind of dog is easily trained.* Errors often occur when these singular nouns are combined with the plural adjectives° *these* and *those: These kinds* (not *kind*) *of dogs are easily trained. Kind, sort,* and *type* should be followed by *of* but not by *a: I don't know what type of* (not *type* or *type of a*) *dog that is.*

 Use *kind of, sort of,* or *type of* only when the word *kind, sort,* or *type* is important: *That was a strange* (not *strange sort of*) *statement.*

lay, lie *Lay* means "put" or "place" and takes a direct object:° *We could lay the tablecloth in the sun.* Its main forms are *lay, laid, laid. Lie* means "recline" or "be situated" and does not take an object: *I lie awake at night. The town lies east of the river.* Its main forms are *lie, lay, lain.*

lead, led The verb *lead* describes present action while *led* describes past action: *I will lead you now to where she once led us.*

less See *fewer, less.*

lie, lay See *lay, lie.*

like, as In formal speech and writing, *like* should not introduce a full clause.° The preferred choice is *as* or *as if: The plan succeeded as* (not *like*) *we hoped.* Use *like* only before a word or phrase: *Other plans like it have failed.*

literally This word means "actually" or "just as the words say," and it should not be used to intensify expressions whose words are not to be taken at face value. The sentence *He was literally climbing the walls* describes a person behaving like an insect, not a person who is restless or anxious. For the latter meaning, *literally* should be omitted.

lōse, loose *Lose* means "mislay": *Did you lose a brown glove? Loose* usually means "unrestrained" or "not tight": *Ann's canary got loose.*

may, can See *can, may.*

may be, maybe *May be* is a verb,° and *maybe* is an adverb° meaning "perhaps": *Tuesday may be a legal holiday. Maybe we won't have classes.*

may of See *have, of.*

media *Media* is the plural of *medium* and takes a plural verb:° *All the news media are increasingly visual.*

might of See *have, of.*

must of See *have, of.*

myself, herself, himself, yourself The *-self* pronouns° refer to or intensify another word or words: *Paul did it himself; Jill herself said so.* In formal speech or writing, avoid using the *-self* pronouns in place of personal pronouns:° *No one except me* (not *myself*) *saw the accident. Michiko and I* (not *myself*) *planned the ceremony.*

nowheres Non-standard for *nowhere.*

number See *amount, number.*

of, have See *have, of.*

OK, O.K., okay All three spellings are acceptable, but avoid this colloquial term in formal speech and writing.

people, persons Except when emphasizing individuals, prefer *people* to *persons: We the people of Canada. . . ; Will the person or persons who saw the accident please notify. . . .*

percent (per cent), percentage Both these terms refer to fractions of one hundred. *Percent* always follows a numeral (*40 percent of the voters*), and the word should be used instead of the symbol (%) in non-technical writing. *Percentage* usually follows an adjective (*a high percentage*).

persons See *people, persons*.

phenomena The plural of *phenomenon* (meaning "perceivable fact" or "unusual occurrence"): *Many phenomena are not recorded. One phenomenon is attracting attention.*

plus *Plus* is standard as a preposition° meaning "in addition to": *His income plus mine is sufficient.* But *plus* is colloquial as a conjunctive adverb:° *Our organization is larger than theirs; moreover* (not *plus*), *we have more money.*

precede, proceed *Precede* means "come before": *My name precedes yours in the alphabet. Proceed* means "move on": *We were told to proceed to the waiting room.*

prejudice, prejudiced *Prejudice* is a noun;° *prejudiced* is an adjective.° Do not drop the *-d* from *prejudiced*: *I was fortunate that my parents were not prejudiced* (not *prejudice*).

principal, principle *Principal* is an adjective° meaning "foremost" or "major," a noun° meaning "chief official," or, in finance, a noun meaning "capital sum." *Principle* is a noun only, meaning "rule" or "axiom." *Her principal reasons for confessing were her principles of right and wrong.*

proceed, precede See *precede, proceed*.

raise, rise *Raise* means "lift" or "bring up" and takes a direct object:° *The Kirks raise cattle.* Its main forms are *raise, raised, raised. Rise* means "get up" and does not take an object: *They must rise at dawn.* Its main forms are *rise, rose, risen.*

real, really In formal speech and writing, *real* should not be used as an adverb;° *really* is the adverb and *real* an adjective.° *Popular reaction to the announcement was really* (not *real*) *enthusiastic.*

reason is because Although colloquially common, this construction should be avoided in formal speech and writing. Use a *that* clause after *reason is: The reason he is absent is that* (not *is because*) *he is sick.* Or: *He is absent because he is sick.*

respectful, respective *Respectful* means "full of (or showing) respect": *Be respectful of other people. Respective* means "separate": *The French and the Germans occupied their respective trenches.*

rise, raise See *raise, rise*.

sensual, sensuous *Sensual* suggests sexuality; *sensuous* means "pleasing to the senses." *Stirred by the sensuous* *scent of meadow grass and flowers, Cheryl and Paul found their thoughts turning* <u>*sensual.*</u>

set, sit *Set* means "put" or "place" and takes a direct object:° *He* <u>*sets*</u> *the pitcher down.* Its main forms are *set, set, set. Sit* means "be seated" and does not take an object: *She* <u>*sits*</u> *on the sofa.* Its main forms are *sit, sat, sat.*

should of See *have, of.*

since *Since* mainly relates to time: *I've been waiting* <u>*since noon.*</u> But *since* is also often used to mean "because": <u>*Since you ask, I'll tell you.*</u> Revise sentences in which the word could have either meaning, such as <u>*Since you left, my life is empty.*</u>

sit, set See *set, sit.*

somebody, some body; someone, some one *Somebody* and *someone* are indefinite pronouns;° *some body* is a noun° modified by *some;* and *some one* is a pronoun° or an adjective° modified by *some.* <u>*Somebody*</u> *ought to invent a shampoo that will give hair* <u>*some body.*</u> <u>*Someone*</u> *told James he should choose* <u>*some one*</u> *plan and stick with it.*

sometime, sometimes, some time *Sometime* means "at an indefinite time in the future": *Why don't you come up and see me* <u>*sometime?*</u> *Sometimes* means "now and then": *I still see my old friend Joe* <u>*sometimes.*</u> *Some time* means "span of time": *I need* <u>*some time*</u> *to make the payments.*

somewheres Non-standard for *somewhere.*

sort of, sort of a See *kind of, sort of, type of.*

supposed to, used to In both these expressions, the *-d* is essential: *I* <u>*used to*</u> (not *use to*) *think so. He's* <u>*supposed to*</u> (not *suppose to*) *meet us.*

sure and, sure to; try and, try to *Sure to* and *try to* are the preferred forms: *Be* <u>*sure to*</u> (not *sure and*) *buy milk.* <u>*Try to*</u> (not <u>*Try and*</u>) *find some decent tomatoes.*

take, bring See *bring, take.*

than, then *Than* is a conjunction° used in comparisons, *then* an adverb° indicating time: *Holmes knew* <u>*then*</u> *that Moriarty was wilier* <u>*than*</u> *he had thought.*

that, which *That* always introduces restrictive clauses:° *We should use the lettuce* <u>*that Susan bought*</u> (*that Susan bought* limits *lettuce* to a particular lettuce). *Which* can introduce both restrictive and non-restrictive clauses,° but many writers reserve *which* only for non-restrictive clauses: *The leftover lettuce,* <u>*which is in the refrigerator,*</u> *would make a good salad* (*which is in the refrigerator* simply provides more information about the lettuce we already know of). Restrictive clauses (with *that* or *which*) are not set off by commas; non-restrictive clauses (with *which*) are. See also pp. 179–80.

their, there, they're *Their* is the possessive° form of *they:* *Give them their money.* *There* indicates place (*I saw her standing there*) or functions as an expletive° (*There is a hole behind you*). *They're* is a contraction° for *they are:* *They're going fast.*

theirselves Non-standard for *themselves.*

then, than See *than, then.*

these kind, these sort, these type, those kind See *kind of, sort of, type of.*

thru A colloquial spelling of *through* that should be avoided in all academic and business writing.

to, too, two *To* is a preposition;° *too* is an adverb° meaning "also" or "excessively"; and *two* is a number. *I too have been to Europe two times.*

toward, towards Both are acceptable, though *toward* is preferred. Use one or the other consistently.

try and, try to See *sure and, sure to; try and, try to.*

type of Don't use *type* without *of: It was a family type of* (not *type*) *restaurant.* Or, better: *It was a family restaurant.* See also *kind of, sort of, type of.*

uninterested See *disinterested, uninterested.*

unique *Unique* means "the only one of its kind" and so cannot sensibly be modified with words such as *very* or *most: That was a unique* (not *a very unique* or *the most unique*) *movie.*

used to See *supposed to, used to.*

wait for, wait on In formal speech and writing, *wait for* means "await" (*I'm waiting for Paul*), and *wait on* means "serve" (*The owner of the store herself waited on us*).

weather, whether The *weather* is the state of the atmosphere. *Whether* introduces alternatives. *The weather will determine whether we go or not.*

well See *good, well.*

whether, if See *if, whether.*

which, who *Which* never refers to people. Use *who* or sometimes *that* for a person or persons and *which* or *that* for a thing or things: *The baby, who was left behind, opened the door, which we had closed.*

who's, whose *Who's* is the contraction° of *who is: Who's at the door? Whose* is the possessive° form of *who: Whose book is that?*

would have Avoid this construction in place of *had* in clauses that begin *if* and state a condition contrary to fact: *If the tree <u>had</u>* (not *<u>would have</u>*) *withstood the fire, it would have been the oldest in town.*

would of See *have, of.*

you In all but very formal writing, *you* is generally appropriate as long as it means "you, the reader." In all writing, avoid indefinite uses of *you,* such as *In one ancient tribe <u>your</u> first loyalty was to <u>your</u> parents.*

your, you're *Your* is the possessive° form of *you: <u>Your</u> dinner is ready. You're* is the contraction° of *you are: <u>You're</u> bound to be late.*

yourself See *myself, herself, himself, yourself.*

Glossary of Terms

This glossary defines the terms and concepts of basic English grammar, including every term marked ° in the text.

absolute phrase A phrase that consists of a noun° or pronoun° plus the *-ing* or *-ed* form of a verb° (a participle°): *Our accommodations arranged, we set out on our trip. They will hire a local person, other things being equal.*

active voice The verb form° used when the sentence subject° names the performer of the verb's action: *The drillers used a rotary blade.* For more, see *voice.*

adjective A word used to modify a noun° or pronoun:° *beautiful morning, ordinary one, good spelling.* Contrast *adverb.* Nouns, word groups, and some verb° forms may also serve as adjectives: *book sale; sale of old books; the sale, which occurs annually; increasing profits.*

adverb A word used to modify a verb,° an adjective,° another adverb, or a whole sentence: *warmly greet* (verb), *only three people* (adjective), *quite seriously* (adverb), *Fortunately, she is employed* (sentence). Word groups may also serve as adverbs: *drove by a farm, plowed the fields when the earth thawed.*

agreement The correspondence of one word to another in person,° number,° or gender.° Mainly, a verb° must agree with its subject° (*The chef orders eggs*), and a pronoun° must agree with it antecedent° (*The chef surveys her breakfast*). See also pp. 49–52 and 58–60.

antecedent The word a pronoun° refers to: *Jonah, who is not yet ten, has already chosen the university he will attend* (*Jonah* is the antecedent of the pronouns *who* and *he*).

appositive A word or word group appearing next to a noun° or pronoun° that renames or identifies it and is equivalent to it: *My brother Michael, the best horn player in town, won the provincial competition* (*Michael* identifies which brother is being referred to; *the best horn player in town* renames *My brother Michael*).

article The words *a, an,* and *the.* Articles always signal that a noun follows. See p. 65 for how to choose between *a* and *an.* See pp. 65–67 for the rules governing *a/an* and *the.*

auxiliary verb See *helping verb.*

case The form of a pronoun° or noun° that indicates its function in the sentence. Most pronouns have three cases.

The SUBJECTIVE CASE is for subjects° and subject comple-ments:° *I, you, he, she, it, we, they, who, whoever.* The OBJ-ECTIVE CASE is for objects:° *me, you, him, her, it, us, them, whom, whomever.* The POSSESSIVE CASE is for ownership: *my/mine, your/yours, his, her/hers, its, our/ours, their/theirs, whose.* Nouns use the subjective form (*dog, Canada*) for all cases except the possessive (*dog's, Canada's*).

clause A group of words containing a subject° and a predi-cate.° A MAIN CLAUSE can stand alone as a sentence: <u>*We can go to the movies*</u>. A SUBORDINATE CLAUSE cannot stand alone as a sentence: *We can go <u>if Julie gets back on time</u>.* For more, see *subordinate clause.*

collective noun A word with singular form that names a group of individuals or things: for instance, *team, army, family, flock, group.* A collective noun generally takes a sin-gular verb and a singular pronoun: *The <u>army is</u> prepared for its role.* See also pp. 50 and 59–60.

comma splice A sentence error in which two sentences (main clauses°) are separated by a comma without *and, but, or, nor,* or another coordinating conjunction.° Splice: *The book was long, it contained useful information.* Re-vised: *The book was long; it contained useful information.* Or: *The book was long, <u>and</u> it contained useful information.* See pp. 72–74.

comparison The form of an adverb° or adjective° that shows its degree of quality or amount. The POSITIVE is the simple, uncompared form: *gross, clumsily.* The COMPARATIVE compares the thing modified to at least one other thing: *grosser, more clumsily.* The SUPERLATIVE indicates that the thing modified exceeds all other things to which it is being compared: *grossest, most clumsily.* The comparative and su-perlative are formed either with the endings *-er* and *-est* or with the words *more* and *most* or *less* and *least.*

complement See *subject complement.*

complex sentence See *sentence.*

compound-complex sentence See *sentence.*

compound construction Two or more words or word groups serving the same function, such as a compound subject° (<u>*Harriet and Peter*</u> *paddled their canoe down the river*), a compound predicate° (*The scout <u>watched and waited</u>*), or a compound sentence (<u>*He smiled, and I laughed*</u>).

compound sentence See *sentence.*

conditional statement A statement expressing a condi-tion contrary to fact and using the subjunctive mood° of the verb: *If she <u>were</u> mayor, the unions would cooperate.*

TERMS

conjunction A word that links and relates parts of a sentence. See *coordinating conjunction* (*and, but,* etc.), *correlative conjunction* (*either... or, both... and,* etc.), and *subordinating conjunction* (*because, if,* etc.).

conjunctive adverb An adverb° that can relate two complete sentences (main clauses°) in a single sentence: *We had hoped to own a house by now; <u>however</u>, prices are still too high.* The main clauses are separated by a semicolon or a period. Some common conjunctive adverbs: *accordingly, also, anyway, besides, certainly, consequently, finally, further, furthermore, hence, however, incidentally, indeed, instead, likewise, meanwhile, moreover, namely, nevertheless, next, nonetheless, now, otherwise, similarly, still, then, thereafter, therefore, thus, undoubtedly.*

contraction A condensed expression, with an apostrophe replacing the missing letters: for example, *doesn't* (*does not*), *we'll* (*we will*).

coordinating conjunction A word linking words or word groups serving the same function: *The dog <u>and</u> cat sometimes fight, <u>but</u> they usually get along.* The coordinating conjunctions are *and, but, or, nor, for, so, yet.*

coordination The linking of words or word groups that are of equal importance, usually with a coordinating conjunction.° *He <u>and</u> I laughed, <u>but</u> she was not amused.* Contrast *subordination.*

correlative conjunction Two or more connecting words that work together to link words or word groups serving the same function: *<u>Both</u> Michiko <u>and</u> June signed up, but <u>neither</u> Stan <u>nor</u> Carlos did.* The correlatives include *both... and, just as... so, not only... but also, not... but, either... or, neither... nor, whether... or, as... as.*

count noun A word that names a person, place, or thing that can be counted (and so may appear in plural form): *camera/cameras, river/rivers, child/children.*

dangling modifier A modifier that does not sensibly describe anything in its sentence. Dangling: *<u>Having arrived late</u>, the concert had already begun.* Revised: *Having arrived late, <u>we found that</u> the concert had already begun.* See p. 169.

determiner A word such as *a, an, the, my,* and *your* that indicates that a noun follows. See also *article.*

direct address A construction in which a word or phrase indicates the person or group spoken to: *Have you finished, <u>John</u>? <u>Farmers</u>, unite.*

direct object A noun° or pronoun° that identifies who or what receives the action of a verb:° *Education opens <u>doors</u>.* For more, see *object* and *predicate.*

direct question A sentence asking a question and concluding with a question mark: *Do they know we are watching?* Contrast *indirect question*.

direct quotation Repetition of what someone has written or said, using the exact words of the original and enclosing them in quotation marks: *Feinberg writes, "The reasons are both obvious and sorry."*

double negative A non-standard form consisting of two negative words used in the same construction so that they effectively cancel each other: *I don't have no money.* Rephrase as *I have no money* or *I don't have any money.*

ellipsis The omission of a word or words from a quotation, indicated by the three spaced periods of an ELLIPSIS MARK: *"It was the best of times, . . . the worst of times."* See also pp. 193–94.

expletive construction A sentence that postpones the subject° by beginning with *there* or *it* and a form of *be*: *It is impossible to get a ticket. There are no more seats available.*

first person See *person*.

fused sentence (run-on sentence) A sentence error in which two complete sentences (main clauses°) are joined with no punctuation or connecting word between them. Fused: *I heard his lecture it was dull.* Revised: *I heard his lecture; it was dull.* See pp. 172–74.

future perfect tense The verb tense expressing an action that will be completed before another future action: *They will have heard by then.* For more, see *tense*.

future tense The verb tense expressing action that will occur in the future: *They will hear soon.* For more, see *tense*.

gender The classification of nouns° or pronouns° as masculine (*he, boy*), feminine (*she, woman*), or neuter (*it, typewriter*).

gerund A verb form that ends in *-ing* and functions as a noun:° *Working is all right for killing time.* For more, see *verbals and verbal phrases*.

gerund phrase See *verbals and verbal phrases*.

helping verb (auxiliary verb) A verb° used with another verb to convey time, possibility, obligation, and other meanings: *You should write a letter. You have written other letters.* The modals are the following: *can, could, may, might, must, ought, shall, should, will, would.* The other helping verbs are forms of *be, have,* and *do*.

idiom An expression that is peculiar to a language and that may not make sense if taken literally: for example, *dark horse, bide your time,* and *by and large*.

TERMS

imperative See *mood*.

indefinite pronoun A word that stands for a noun° and does not refer to a specific person or thing: *all, any, anybody, anyone, anything, each, either, everybody, everyone, everything, neither, nobody, none, no one, nothing, one, some, somebody, someone, something.* Indefinite pronouns usually take singular verbs and are referred to by singular pronouns (*something makes its presence felt*). See also pp. 59, 61–62.

indicative See *mood*.

indirect object A noun° or pronoun° that identifies to whom or what something is done: *Give them the award.* For more, see *object* and *predicate*.

indirect question A sentence reporting a question and ending with a period: *Writers wonder if their work must always be lonely.* Contrast *direct question*.

indirect quotation A report of what someone has written or said, but not using the exact words of the original and not enclosing the words in quotation marks. Quotation: *"The medium is the message."* Indirect quotation: *Marshall McLuhan said that the medium was the message.*

infinitive A verb form° consisting of the verb's dictionary form plus *to: to swim, to write.* For more, see *verbals and verbal phrases*.

infinitive phrase See *verbals and verbal phrases*.

intensive pronoun See *pronoun*.

interjection A word standing by itself or inserted in a construction to exclaim or command attention: *Hey! Ouch! What the heck did you do that for?*

interrogative pronoun See *pronoun*.

intransitive verb A verb° that does not require a following word (direct object°) to complete its meaning: *Mosquitoes buzz. The hospital may close.* For more, see *predicate*.

irregular verb See *verb forms*.

linking verb A verb that links, or connects, a subject° and a word that renames or describes the subject (a subject complement°): *They are golfers. You seem lucky.* The linking verbs are the forms of *be*, the verbs of the senses (*look, sound, smell, feel, taste*), and a few others (*appear, become, grow, prove, remain, seem, turn*). For more, see *predicate*.

main clause A word group that contains a subject° and a predicate,° does not begin with a subordinating word, and may stand alone as a sentence: *The president was not overbearing.* For more, see *clause*.

main verb The part of a verb phrase° that carries the principal meaning: *had been* <u>*walking*</u>, *could* <u>*happen*</u>, *was* <u>*chilled*</u>. Contrast *helping verb*.

misplaced modifier A modifier so far from the term it modifies or so close to another term it could modify that its relation to the rest of the sentence is unclear. Misplaced: *The children played with firecrackers that they bought illegally <u>in the field</u>.* Revised: *The children played <u>in the field</u> with firecrackers that they bought illegally.*

modal See *helping verb*.

modifier Any word or word group that limits or qualifies the meaning of another word or word group. Modifiers include adjectives° and adverbs° as well as words and word groups that act as adjectives and adverbs.

mood The form of a verb° that shows how the speaker views the action. The INDICATIVE MOOD, the most common, is used to make statements or ask questions: *The play <u>will be performed</u> Saturday. <u>Did</u> you <u>get</u> tickets?* The IMPERATIVE MOOD gives a command: *Please <u>get</u> good seats. <u>Avoid</u> the top balcony.* The SUBJUNCTIVE MOOD expresses a wish, a condition contrary to fact, a recommendation, or a request: *I wish George <u>were coming</u> with us. If he <u>were</u> here, he'd come.*

non-count noun A word that names a person, place, or thing and that is not considered countable in English (and so does not appear in plural form): *confidence, information, silver, work.*

non-restrictive clause See *non-restrictive element*.

non-restrictive element A word or word group that does not limit the word it refers to and that is not essential to the meaning of the sentence. Non-restrictive elements are usually set off by commas: *Sleep, <u>which we all need</u>, occupies a third of our lives. His wife, <u>Patricia</u>, is a chemist.* Contrast *restrictive element*.

noun A word that names a person, place, thing, quality, or idea: *Maggie, Alberta, clarinet, satisfaction, socialism.* See also *collective noun, count noun, non-count noun,* and *proper noun.*

noun clause See *subordinate clause*.

number The form of a word that indicates whether it is singular or plural. Singular: *I, he, this, child, runs, hides.* Plural: *we, they, these, children, run, hide.*

object A noun° or pronoun° that receives the action of or is influenced by another word. A DIRECT OBJECT receives the action of a verb° or verbal° and usually follows it in a sentence: *We watched the <u>stars</u>.* An INDIRECT OBJECT tells for or to whom something is done: *Reiner bought <u>us</u> tapes.* An

OBJECT OF A PREPOSITION usually follows a preposition° and is linked by it to the rest of the sentence: *They are going to Montreal for the jazz festival.*

objective case The form of a pronoun° when it is the object° of a verb° (*call him*) or the object of a preposition° (*for us*). For more, see *case.*

object of preposition See *object.*

parallelism Similarity of grammatical form between two or more coordinated elements: *Rising prices and declining incomes left many people in bad debt and worse despair.* See pp. 23–25.

parenthetical expression A word or construction that interrupts a sentence and is not part of its main structure, called *parenthetical* because it could (or does) appear in parentheses: *Emily Carr (1871–1945) was a Canadian painter. Her work, incidentally, is in the museum.*

participial phrase See *verbals and verbal phrases.*

participle See *verbals and verbal phrases.*

particle A preposition° or adverb° in a two-word verb: *catch on, look up.*

parts of speech The classes into which words are commonly grouped according to their form, function, and meaning: nouns, pronouns, verbs, adjectives, adverbs, conjunctions, prepositions, and interjections. See separate entries for each part of speech.

passive voice The verb form° used when the sentence subject° names the receiver of the verb's action: *The mixture was stirred.* For more, see *voice.*

past participle The *-ed* form of most verbs:° *fished, hopped.* Some verbs form their past participles in irregular ways: *begun, written.* For more, see *verbals and verbal phrases* and *verb forms.*

past perfect tense The verb tense expressing an action that was completed before another past action: *No one had heard that before.* For more, see *tense.*

past tense The verb tense expressing action that occurred in the past: *Everyone laughed.* For more, see *tense.*

past-tense form The verb form used to indicate action that occurred in the past, usually created by adding *-d* or *-ed* to the verb's dictionary form (*smiled*) but created differently for most irregular verbs (*began, threw*). For more, see *verb forms.*

perfect tenses The verb tenses indicating action completed before another specific time or action: *have walked, had walked, will have walked.* For more, see *tense.*

person The form of a verb° or pronoun° that indicates whether the subject is speaking, spoken to, or spoken about. In the FIRST PERSON the subject is speaking: *I am, we are*. In the SECOND PERSON the subject is spoken to: *you are*. In the THIRD PERSON the subject is spoken about: *he/she/it is, they are*.

personal pronoun *I, you, he, she, it, we,* or *they:* a word that substitutes for a specific noun° or other pronoun. For more, see *case*.

phrase A group of related words that lacks a subject° or a predicate° or both: *She ran into the field. She tried to jump the fence.* See also *absolute phrase, prepositional phrase, verbals and verbal phrases*.

plain form The dictionary form of a verb: *buy, make, run, swivel*. For more, see *verb forms*.

plural More than one. See *number*.

positive form See *comparison*.

possessive case The form of a noun° or pronoun° that indicates its ownership of something else: *men's attire, your briefcase*. For more, see *case*.

predicate The part of a sentence that makes an assertion about the subject.° The predicate may consist of an intransitive verb° (*The earth trembled*), a transitive verb° plus direct object° (*The earthquake shook buildings*), a linking verb° plus subject complement° (*The result was chaos*), a transitive verb plus indirect object° and direct object (*The government sent the city aid*), or a transitive verb plus direct object and object complement (*the citizens considered the earthquake a disaster*).

preposition A word that forms a noun° or pronoun° (plus any modifiers) into a PREPOSITIONAL PHRASE: *about love, down the steep stairs*. The common prepositions: *about, above, according to, across, after, against, along, along with, among, around, as, at, because of, before, behind, below, beneath, beside, between, beyond, by, concerning, despite, down, during, except, except for, excepting, for, from, in, in addition to, inside, in spite of, instead of, into, like, near, next to, of, off, on, onto, out, out of, outside, over, past, regarding, since, through, throughout, till, to, toward, under, underneath, unlike, until, up, upon, with, within, without*.

prepositional phrase A word group consisting of a preposition° and its object.° Prepositional phrases usually serve as adjectives° (*We saw a movie about sorrow*) and as adverbs° (*We went back for the second show*).

present participle The *-ing* form of a verb:° *swimming, flying*. For more, see *verbals and verbal phrases*.

present perfect tense The verb tense expressing action that began in the past and is linked to the present: *Dogs have buried bones here before.* For more, see *tense.*

present tense The verb tense expressing action that is occurring now, occurs habitually, or is generally true: *Dogs bury bones here often.* For more, see *tense.*

principal parts The three forms of a verb from which its various tenses are created: the PLAIN FORM (*stop, go*), the PAST-TENSE FORM (*stopped, went*), and the PAST PARTICIPLE (*stopped, gone*). For more, see *tense* and *verb forms.*

progressive tenses The verb tenses that indicate continuing (progressive) action and use the *-ing* form of the verb: *A dog was burying a bone here this morning.* For more, see *tense.*

pronoun A word used in place of a noun,° such as *I, he, everyone, who,* and *herself.* See also *indefinite pronoun, personal pronoun, relative pronoun.*

proper noun A word naming a specific person, place, or thing and beginning with a capital letter: *Peter Mansbridge, Mount Robson, Ottawa, Canada Post.*

regular verb See *verb forms.*

relative pronoun *Who, whoever, which,* or *that:* a word that relates a group of words to a noun° or other pronoun:° *Ask the woman who knows all. This may be the question that stumps her.* For more, see *case.*

restrictive clause See *restrictive element.*

restrictive element A word or word group that is essential to the meaning of the sentence because it limits the word it refers to: removing it would leave the meaning unclear or too general. Restrictive elements are *not* set off by commas: *Dorothy's companion the Scarecrow lacks a brain. The man who called about the apartment said he'd try again.* Contrast *non-restrictive element.*

run-on sentence See *fused sentence.*

-s form See *verb forms.*

second person See *person.*

sentence A complete unit of thought, consisting of at least a subject° and a predicate° that are not introduced by a subordinating word. Sentences can be classed on the basis of their structure: A SIMPLE SENTENCE contains one main clause:° *I'm leaving.* A COMPOUND SENTENCE contains at least two main clauses: *I'd like to stay, but I'm leaving.* A COMPLEX SENTENCE contains one main clause and at least one subordinate clause:° *If you let me go now, you'll be sorry.* A COMPOUND-COMPLEX SENTENCE contains at least two main clauses and at least one subordinate clause: *I'm leaving because you want me to, but I'd rather stay.*

sentence fragment A sentence error in which a group of words is set off as a sentence even though it begins with a subordinating word or lacks a subject° or a predicate° or both. Fragment: *She was not in shape for the race. <u>Which she had hoped to win</u>*. Revised: *She was not in shape for the race, which she had hoped to win.* See pp. 71–72.

series Three or more items with the same function: *We gorged on <u>bacon, eggs, and potatoes</u>.*

simple sentence See *sentence*.

simple tenses See *tense*.

singular One. See *number*.

split infinitive The usually awkward interruption of an infinitive° and its marker *to* by a modifier: *Management decided <u>to not introduce</u> the new product.* See p. 168.

squinting modifier A modifier that could modify the words on either side of it: *The plan we considered <u>seriously</u> worries me.*

subject In grammar, the part of a sentence that names something and about which an assertion is made in the predicate:° *The quick, brown <u>fox</u> jumped lazily* (simple subject); *<u>The quick, brown fox</u> jumped lazily* (complete subject).

subject complement A word that renames or describes the subject° of a sentence, after a linking verb:° *The stranger was a <u>man</u>* (noun°). *He seemed <u>gigantic</u>* (adjective°).

subjective case The form of a pronoun° when it is the subject° of a sentence (*<u>I</u> called*) or a subject complement° (*It was <u>I</u>*). For more, see *case*.

subjunctive See *mood*.

subordinate clause A word group that consists of a subject° and a predicate,° begins with a subordinating word such as *because* or *who*, and is not a question: *They voted for <u>whoever seemed to care the least because they mistrusted politicians</u>.* Subordinate clauses may serve as adjectives° (*The car <u>that hit Fred</u> was running a red light*), as adverbs° (*The car hit Fred <u>when it ran a red light</u>*), or as nouns° (*<u>Whoever was driving</u> should be arrested*). Subordinate clauses may *not* serve as complete sentences.

subordinating conjunction A word that forms a complete sentence into a word group (a subordinate clause°) that can serve as an adverb° or a noun.° *Everyone was relieved <u>when</u> the meeting ended.* Some common subordinating conjunctions: *after, although, as, as if, as long as, as though, because, before, even if, even though, if, if only, in order that, now that, once, rather than, since, so that, than, that, though, till, unless, until, when, whenever, where, whereas, wherever, while.*

subordination The use of grammatical structures to de-emphasize one element in a sentence by making it dependent on rather than equal to another element. Through subordination, *I left six messages; the doctor failed to call* becomes <u>*Although I left six messages*</u>, *the doctor failed to call* or <u>*After six messages*</u>, *the doctor failed to call.*

tag question A question attached to the end of a statement and composed of a pronoun,° a helping verb,° and sometimes the word *not: It isn't raining,* <u>*is it*</u>? *It is sunny,* <u>*isn't it*</u>?

tense The form of a verb° that expresses the time of its action, usually indicated by the verb's endings and by helping verbs. See also *verb forms.*

Present   Action that is occurring now, occurs habitually, or is generally true

Simple present	Present progressive
Plain form or *-s* form	*Am, is,* or *are* plus *-ing* form
I *walk.*	I *am walking.*
You/we/they *walk.*	You/we/they *are walking.*
He/she/it *walks.*	He/she/it *is walking.*

Past   Action that occurred before now

Simple past	Past progressive
Past-tense form (*-d* or *-ed*)	*Was* or *were* plus *-ing* form
I/he/she/it *walked.*	I/he/she/it *was walking.*
You/we/they *walked.*	You/we/they *were walking.*

Future   Action that will occur in the future

Simple future	Future progressive
Will plus plain form	*Will be* plus *-ing* form
I/you/he/she/it/we/. they *will walk*	I/you/he/she/it/we/ they *will be walking.*

Present perfect   Action that began in the past and is linked to the present

Present perfect	Present perfect progressive
Have or *has* plus past participle (*-d* or *-ed*)	*Have been* or *has been* plus *-ing* form
I/you/we/they *have walked.*	I/you/we/they *have been walking.*
He/she/it *has walked.*	He/she/it *has been walking.*

Past perfect   Action that was completed before another past action

Past perfect	Past perfect progressive
Had plus past participle (*-d* or *-ed*)	*Had been* plus *-ing* form
I/you/he/she/it/we/they *had walked.*	I/you/he/she/it/we/they *had been walking.*

Future perfect   Action that will be completed before another future action

Future perfect	Future perfect progressive
Will have plus past participle (*-d* or *-ed*)	*Will have been* plus *-ing* form
I/you/he/she/it/we/they *will have walked.*	I/you/he/she/it/we/they *will have been walking.*

transitional expression A word or phrase that links sentences and shows the relations between them. Transitional expressions can signal the following: addition or sequence (*also, besides, finally, first, furthermore, in addition, last*); comparison (*also, likewise, similarly*); contrast (*even so, however, in contrast, nevertheless, still*); examples (*for example, for instance, specifically, that is*); intensification (*indeed, in fact, of course, truly*); place (*below, elsewhere, here, nearby, to the east*); time (*afterward, at last, earlier, immediately, meanwhile, shortly, simultaneously*); repetition or summary (*all in all, in brief, in other words, in short, in summary, that is*); and cause and effect (*as a result, consequently, hence, otherwise, therefore, thus*).

transitive verb A verb° that requires a following word (a direct object°) to complete its meaning: *We raised the roof.* For more, see *predicate.*

verb A word that expresses an action (*bring, change*), an occurrence (*happen, become*), or a state of being (*be, seem*). A verb is the essential word in a predicate,° the part of a sentence that makes an assertion about the subject.° With endings and helping verbs,° verbs can indicate tense,° mood,° voice,° number,° and person.° For more, see separate entries for each of these aspects as well as *verb forms.*

verbals and verbal phrases VERBALS are verb forms used as adjectives,° adverbs,° or nouns.° They form VERBAL PHRASES with objects° and modifiers. A PRESENT PARTICIPLE adds *-ing* to the dictionary form of a verb (*living*). A PAST PARTICIPLE usually adds *-d* or *-ed* to the dictionary form (*lived*), although irregular verbs form the past participle in other ways (*begun, swept*). A participle or PARTICIPIAL PHRASE usually serves as an adjective: *Strolling shoppers fill the malls.* A GERUND is the *-ing* form of a verb used as a noun. Gerunds and GERUND PHRASES can do whatever nouns can do: *Shopping satisfies personal needs.* An INFINITIVE is the verb's dictionary form plus *to: to live.* Infinitives and INFINITIVE PHRASES may serve as nouns (*To design a mall is to create an artificial environment*), as adverbs (*Malls are designed to make shoppers feel safe*), or as adjectives (*The environment supports the impulse to shop*).

Note that a verbal *cannot* serve as the only verb in the predicate° of a sentence. For that, it requires a helping verb:° *Shoppers were strolling.*

verb forms Verbs have five distinctive forms. The PLAIN FORM is the dictionary form: *A few artists <u>live</u> in town today*. The *-s* FORM adds *-s* or *-es* to the plain form: *The artist <u>lives</u> in town today*. The PAST-TENSE FORM usually adds *-d* or *-ed* to the plain form: *Many artists <u>lived</u> in town before this year*. Some verbs' past-tense forms are irregular, such as *began, fell, swam, threw, wrote*. The PAST PARTICIPLE is usually the same as the past-tense form, although, again, some verbs' past participles are irregular (*begun, fallen, swum, thrown, written*). The PRESENT PARTICIPLE adds *-ing* to the plain form: *A few artists are <u>living</u> in town today*.

Regular verbs are those that add *-d* or *-ed* to the plain form for the past-tense form and past participle. Irregular verbs create these forms in irregular ways (see above).

verb phrase See *phrase*. A verb° of more than one word that serves as the predicate° of a sentence: *The movie has started*.

voice The form of a verb° that tells whether the sentence subject° performs the action or is acted upon. In the ACTIVE VOICE the subject acts: *The Province <u>controls</u> rents*. In the PASSIVE VOICE the subject is acted upon: *Rents <u>are controlled</u> by the Province*. The actor in a passive sentence may be stated (*the Province*) or not stated: *Rents <u>are controlled</u>*. See also pp. 147–49.

Index

Editing Symbols

Your readers may use some of these symbols to mark editing you should do. Page numbers refer you to relevant sections of this handbook.